Understanding and Transforming the Black Church

understanding
&

transforming

the black
church

ANTHONY B. PINN

CASCADE *Books* · Eugene, Oregon

Cascade Books
An Imprint of Wipf and Stock Publishers
199 W. 8th Ave., Suite 3
Eugene, OR 97401

www.wipfandstock.com

ISBN 13: 978-1-55635-301-7

Cataloging-in-Publication data:

Pinn, Anthony B.

    Understanding and transforming the black church / Anthony B. Pinn.

    ISBN 13: 978-1-55635-301-7

    xx + 146 p. ; 23 cm. Includes bibliographical references and index.

    1. African Americans—Religion. 2. Black theology. I. Title.

BT82.7 P56 2010

Manufactured in the U.S.A.

Dedicated to

Ms. Juanita Berry and the Ancestors

Contents

Acknowledgments

BOOK PROJECTS COME TO scholars in a variety of ways, and with differing levels of urgency. This project first surfaced as a possibility during a visit with dear friends, Juan and Stacey Floyd-Thomas. And while the final product does not fully mirror the contours of that initial conversation, it was over dinner one evening they suggested I write a book that collected some of my thinking on the Black Church—a project that spoke to why I continue my interest in Black churches although I no longer belong to one. I am thankful to Juan and Stacey for their acts of kindness and compassion, as well as for their insightful and challenging feedback on an early version of this book. They are friends and family, and I am grateful.

I am grateful to James H. Cone for hours of conversation during which he gave me opportunity to think through many of the issues addressed in this volume. I appreciate the rigorous debate and encouragement I received during those meetings. I am also thankful to Peter Paris and Katie Cannon for their keen insights, encouragement, and critical engagement of my work over the years. They have been good friends and mentors. My explicit and implicit attention to their work and their challenges to my thinking in this book is meant as a sign of my deep and abiding respect and appreciation for their wise counsel and inspiring scholarship. Cheryl Townsend Gilkes provided important insight concerning many of the points made in chapter 6. Thank you.

I would also like to express my gratitude to friends and colleagues at Rice University and elsewhere for their encouragement, critique, and good humor. In particular, Caroline Levander read an early version of this book and provided important suggestions for improving the arguments. Michael Emerson provided statistical information for several of the chapters, thank you. Alexander Byrd and Edward Cox provided good humor and lunchtime conversation that helped in a variety of ways. Benjamin Hall listened to some of the arguments found in several chapters, and he provided sharp insights. Thank you. As always my brothers—Hakim Lucas, Benjamin Valentin, Eli Valentin, and Ramon Rentas—offer friendship and support that keeps me balanced.

Though started some time ago, this book was finished during a sabbatical from Rice University (spring 2009), and I appreciate the support Rice University demonstrated by granting that time away from my classroom. Although I was not in the classroom, my graduate students continued their good questions and comments, all of which helped this and other projects along. The staff at Wipf and Stock Publishers has shown me support and patience over the past several years; and, I thank them all.

This book is a collection of new materials and previously published essays. Because arguments and projects build on early efforts, the ways in which some themes here are framed and phrased reflects other writings in places such as *Religious Humanism, Theological Education,* and *the AME Church Review.* However, I have drawn more heavily and more fully from some previously published pieces (presented here with some alterations) first presented in *Religious Studies Review, Black Theology: An International Journal,* and *Religion Dispatches.* Full acknowledgement information on the use of these materials is found at the start of the corresponding chapters. In addition, I gratefully acknowledge formal permission to reprint other materials: chapter 5 was published as "Martin Luther King, Jr.'s God, Humanist Sensibilities, and Moral Evil," in *Theology Today* 65 (2008) 57–66, and it is used here by permission of *Theology Today.* Chapter 3 first appeared as "Peoples Temple as Black Religion: Re-Imagining the Contours of Black Religious Studies," in *Peoples Temple and Black Religion in America,* edited by Rebecca Moore et al. (Indiana University Press, 2004) 1–27; it is reprinted with permission of Indiana University Press. I have included previously published material because here it finds a new audience and intent as well as an alternate framing not presented before. Also, these materials are presented here because they advance the purposes of this book in important ways. These pieces combined with the new chapters are more than the sum of their parts; they represent a discussion I have not developed elsewhere in my writings. It is my hope that taken together they respond to longstanding questions and challenges to some of my thinking on Black religion in general and the Black Church in particular.

Finally, working on this project brought to mind the support and assistance I received during my time in New York City—a period of my life when many of the transitions in my thinking took place. (I still think of NYC as "home.") Bridge Street AME Church was the central location for this examination of my religious commitments as connected to my academic pursuits. Friends and family (particularly my sister Melinda Howard and brother Jesse Howard) at Bridge Street made those years productive. Thank you. In particular, Ms. Juanita Berry, the church office administrator, was kind beyond belief. She encouraged my coursework and celebrated my efforts in ministry. (I don't think she missed one of my sermons given during the 6:30 AM service.) So many afternoons she let me take time away from my work-study job to read and ask questions. It was in her office that I opened Cornel West's *Prophesy Deliverance!* and James Cone's *A Black Theology of Liberation*. Over the years I have lost contact with Ms. Berry, but she has always been in my thoughts. I am grateful for her support, and it is to Ms. Berry that I dedicate this book. I doubt she will agree with most of my conclusions and she may be troubled by elements of my perspective. But, I hope she will see in this book the freedom to think and "be" she nurtured more than twenty years ago. While some of the ideas in this book may not be to her liking, I hope my appreciation for her will make her smile.

Introduction

LIKE SO MANY OTHERS, I spent my early years in Black churches—Wednesdays and weekends full of church-centered activities. Life revolved around geography of commitment defined by the grammar and vocabulary of Black Christianity and housed within the confines of a clearly religious world. There were various tracks of involvement, a range of a/vocational opportunities presented. After a short period of time, I selected the ministry and began my training early by reading Scripture, leading prayers, and lining hymns. With time I took that training further by preaching my trial sermon and formally entering church ministry. My first year of college ended with me ordained a deacon in the African Methodist Episcopal Church. There was for me, I believe, a promising career. However, I eventually left ordained ministry.

What that departure entailed was a shift in my personal, religious commitments. It did not and does not connote hostility toward Black churches. It does not entail a desire to close the doors and condemn the vision of Black churches.

My ongoing interest in the Black Church is at times met with surprise. "But . . . you don't believe in God," is often the response. While that statement suggests a good reason for me not adhering to ordination and not seeking vocational goals involving church ministry, I believe it says little concerning proper criteria for academic research related to these churches.

On occasions when I am met with those words, I make the obligatory effort to explain my perception of the academic study of Black religion (and Black churches in particular) over against the priestly function of ministers—noting the obvious: one need not be a practicing member of a faith in order to thoughtfully and productively study it and produce reasonable scholarship about it. Suspicion concerning my motives is seldom abated by apologetics. My departure from the Black Church and my embrace of Religious Humanism cast a rather large theological and ideological shadow.

My interest in discussing the Black Church and my tenacious hold to the label *theologian* cause a type of vocational dissonance. It seems for some that there is, in my departure from the Black Church, an element of betrayal, or at least a surrender of the insider position they mark as necessary for authentic and legitimate study and discussion of the church: "You left it . . . so leave it alone!"

Mine is a position betwixt and between, representing closeness to the Black Church—based on an understanding of its workings—but also a distance from it in that I do not personally hold to its theological assumptions. This posture involves a creative tension between description of the positive workings of a religious orientation (in this case the Black Church) and critique of the shortcomings and inconsistencies of a religious orientation. What this position does not require is personal adherence. Does it not make some sense to locate the commonality of African American theologians not in a particular faith community but within a more general "tradition of political struggle and cultural and religious resistance to oppression."[1]

Restrictions on who speaks about Black churches and what they should say seems an odd development in light of what at the time was an encouraging comment based on a call for comparative religion strategies made by leading scholar Dwight Hopkins, who wrote: "Because Christianity, though the dominant form, is not an exclusive faith reflection in black life, we need methods of comparing other expressions of ultimate convictions."[2] However, outside the realm of the abstract and with regard to my particular case, Hopkins also notes when reviewing *Why, Lord? Suffering and Evil in Black Theology*: "Pinn also calls for broadening the conversation around evil and suffering to include his voice of non-theistic humanism. But his position seems to deny the existence of God and claims that anyone believing in any positive reality to suffering is wrong and dangerous for the betterment of oppressed black humanity. Given his conclusion and instructions regarding the way forward for black liberation, what motivation is there for someone holding the condemned contrary position to enter into dialogue with Pinn's viewpoint?"[3]

---

1. West, *Prophesy Deliverance!* 117.

2. Hopkins, *Shoes That Fit Our Feet*, 216.

3. Hopkins, review of Anthony B. Pinn's *Why, Lord?* 514–16.

Why, Lord? was my first book, and it entailed my effort to create a space of engagement by arguing for the legitimacy of Religious Humanism's place in the religious geography of African American communities.

I challenged a particular dimension of Black Christian thought and problematized its ability to secure the liberation promised. I had not and have not, as far as I am concerned, denied the reality and legitimacy of Black churches. Rather I have both celebrated and critiqued these institutions *as* an unapologetic Humanist. Why would resistance from a Humanist render impossible discourse with other academics? *Why, Lord?* was polemical in a certain way—involving normative claims and firm positions and opinions. Yet, it should be remembered that book responded to a range of normative claims and firm positions/opinions regarding Black Christianity—including the assumption by many that Black Christianity and the Black community are synonymous in significant ways. This imperialist position of the Black Church held by some colleagues was considered justified because of Christianity's numerical and theological dominance.

The problem, however, ultimately may not be a matter of theological perspective; but rather a matter of communal identity. Cornel West speaks to this point when saying, "the social dimension of the freedom predominant in Black Christianity does not primarily concern political struggle, but rather cultural solidarity. The politics of the Black Church is highly ambiguous, with a track record of widespread opportunism. Yet the cultural practices of the Black Church embody a basic reality— sustained Black solidarity in the midst of a hostile society." According to this schema, in leaving the church, I had rejected the logic of solidarity and, as a consequence, had become unrecognizable as a theologian and as a commentator on the Black Church.[4]

What is more, my embrace of a marginal tradition, by extension, justified questions (and in some cases dismissals) concerning my ability and motivation for discussing Black churches.[5] In light of this orientation,

---

4. West, "Subversive Joy and Revolutionary Patience in Black Christianity," 437.

5. One might find some reason for this posture from those who have as a primary consideration the building and preservation of Black churches—full-time ministers and involved laity—particularly those with limited contact with the academy and its workings. As J. Alfred Smith Sr. remarks, "I believe that too many pastors are anti-intellectuals who cease growing as students upon graduation from seminary." This, nonetheless, is not the full extent of the issue at hand; it cannot be isolated with any benefit to a vague group of anti-intellectual ministers when there are counter examples of engaged and

some struggle to determine where I "fit" in the discussion of Black churches in light of my alternate religious commitment. By way of response, I say
I am a man of faith but simply a different (but no less important) faith.
My take on Black churches involves an insider view based on past history and continued exposure, as well as an outsider orientation because
Christian claims are not embraced as my personal orientation. I suggest
that critique of Black churches is a necessary component of deep regard as
is love for those institutions. Implicit here is a reorientation, an alternate
cartography of appreciation which is marked by affirmation couched in a
call for accountability and responsibility on the part of Black churches. It
is a measuring of these institutions against the claims they make and the
outcomes produced.

Cutting to the chase, the work performed by this book is done on
the margins, but as has been said often the margins can serve as a "space"
of insight and perspective.[6] This positioning on the margin does not
disqualify me from study of and commentary on the Black Church. To
the contrary, the margin provides a somewhat unique take on the Black
Church, allowing for a much fuller view of its workings—both elements
worthy of celebration as well as elements needing critique and correction.
Mindful of this, the various chapters address two primary concerns drawn
from the title of the book. The first three chapters address issues related
to how one might understand the Black Church. That is to say, they give
attention to the "look" of the Black Church as well as the position of the
scholar of Black religion to the Black Church. In chapter 1 I am concerned
with discussion of the Black bodies found within the pews. This concern
is expressed first through a description of how two leading theologians
who explicitly address issues of embodiment, Kelly Brown Douglas and
Dwight Hopkins, (re)present and understand Christian Black bodies.

In the second chapter I am concerned with an effort to unpack the
position of the scholar of Black religion to the Black Church. Here I am
concerned with an effort to unpack the assumed need for an "insider" perspective on the Black Church. I argue this position often loses its critical

---

informed ministers willing to dialogue. The degree of anti-intellectualism and fear of
critique within Black churches can be debated and perhaps rationalized in a variety of
ways. However, less reasonable (and perhaps bad form) is a similar failure by those who
have as a primary obligation intellectual interrogation of religious thinking and practice
(Smith, "Black Theology and the Parish Ministry," 90).

6. For parallels to this statement on a larger religio-political scale, see Pinn, "Inauguration Day," para. 1–8.

edge through an effort to work from the context of African American Christianity's self understanding. That is to say, this insider orientation runs the risk of speaking for Black churches in ways that compromise the possibility of critically engaging and assessing Black churches for fear of being ostracized. What I push instead is critical engagement of the church, sustained discussion of these churches—their nature and meaning—related to a set of criteria, none of which involve personal allegiance. Hence I suggest the purpose of scholarship on Black churches is not the affirmation of those churches, but rather a high level of discourse meant to address the nature and meaning of those institutions. In turn, churches might use this information to further refine their thought and practice. So conceived, the first order of business for the scholar of Black churches is not a response to the "how do I preach this?" question. Instead there ought to be recognition that this question can often serve as a prophylactic against critique and change—becoming a way to blur the line between the priestly role of churches and the potentially "prophetic" tone of scholarship.

The third chapter in this section serves to interrogate the assumed understanding of the theological arrangement and belief/practice structures of Black churches. It does so by exploring the manner in which these assumptions regarding the form and content of Black churches might be challenged through attention to organizations such as Peoples Temple. The goal is to recognize the existence of Black churches within a complex religious terrain. Furthermore, this chapter promotes an understanding of Black churches as not reified institutions but rather institutions with porous boundaries. By suggesting these two conclusions, this chapter serves to better limit and measure the degree to which the assumed Black Church is used as the litmus test for all African American religiosity.

The first section of the book is meant to provide cartography of the Black Church—the nature of its membership and the troubles associated with studying it. In this way, these three chapters seek to trouble the assumed essential nature of Black Church membership and scholarship by showing the diversity and inconsistencies that mark the Black Church. By outlining its membership as well as the nature of scholarship on these churches, this first section affords perspective and a framing of Black churches that recognizes their limits and also their multidimensionality. Chapters 1 and 2 provide a way of approaching the Black Church, and chapter 3 demonstrates the "pay off" of this approach by reexamining

Peoples Temple—an organization seldom mentioned in Black Church Studies—for what it tells about the nature and meaning of Black Church thought and practice. Once the Black Church is so framed, there is greater opportunity to productively wrestle with some of its more vexing problems.

The second section of the book tackles three significant issues that have plagued Black churches for centuries—the nature/meaning of Black bodies, the problem of moral evil, and gender-based discrimination. In short, this section proposes three ways in which Black churches might be transformed and improved through creative attention to these three issues. As the arguments are developed, attention is given to what Black churches have done up to this point in history to address these concerns as well as what might serve as new strategies. In the first of the three chapters, I problematize the perception and "placement" of Black bodies in churches in light of discriminatory practices marking the public arenas of life. And I offer thoughts on how Black churches address this challenge to the well-being of the Black bodies that populated houses of worship. The second chapter wrestles with moral evil in light of the critique of Black religious thought offered by William R. Jones better than thirty years ago. I conclude in that chapter that Black churches have a way of maintaining the "real" nature of human suffering while also affirming the most essential elements of their god concept. Using Martin Luther King Jr.'s theological background, I provide a blueprint of this alternate response to moral evil. Finally, I address the nagging problem of gender-based discrimination in Black churches. In that chapter I push for a move beyond theological argument and biblical precedence as the grounds for countering gender-based restriction on church leadership. Instead I push for a strategy that involves clear thinking on how to secure greater opportunities through a withholding of resources until change takes place. As a matter of context, I must note that gender-based discrimination is not a dilemma unique to Black churches. However, the self-understanding and history of Black churches, along with the somewhat unique social positioning of its members give gender discrimination a certain "look and footprint." If the liberative claims of Black churches are to be achieved, creative attention to gender-based discrimination is necessary.

Following this section is a concluding reflection on President Barack Obama's representation of the shifting nature of religious commitment as political practice. It is my hope these final thoughts will serve as a prolegomenon of sorts, an opportunity to think through the Black Church's changed relationship to federal politics in the post–George W. Bush era represented by the dawning of President Barack Obama's administration. There is great potential for reworking public life and framing the input of religious communities in public debate marking President Obama's administration. However, I place the potentially positive impact of Black churches on pressing problems of our day within the context of the failings of Black churches with regard to these very issues.

What I hope to offer through the six chapters and the concluding reflection comprising this volume is an explicit discussion of key concerns related to the study of Black churches, as well as an implicit response to critics who question how and why a "nonbeliever" would discuss Black churches. In this way these chapters (new and previously published) involve an intellectual synergy that offers a different angle on my scholarship as it relates to Black churches. My marginal status, I assert, affords a perspective on the nature and working of Black churches unavailable to its affiliates. I would go so far as to say, this position on the margins allows clear sight on some issues and practices more difficult to see and explore from within. This book offers perspective, a view of Black churches that recognizes the overlap between the African American community and Black churches, but also rejects assumptions that these two are identical constituencies. By keeping in perspective the parameters of Black churches, one is better able to assess the work of Black churches.

Once an insider, I remain steadfast in my belief that my celebration and critique of the Black Church tradition at its best (and worst) remains thoughtful and accurate. I am not a member of a Black Church, but I have not forgotten the workings of Black Christian faith. My movement away from church membership, away from the ordained ministry, meant in some church circles that I was no longer family, or at best I was now the odd "cousin" no one talks about. What this demotion in status fails to consider is this: I remain interested in and appreciative of the Black Church—the *best* of its thought and action—and I continue to reflect on this religious institution in ways I believe to be reasonable, responsible, and thoughtfully critical.

It is my hope that this book will stimulate conversation, and provide opportunity for new approaches to old issues.

Part I

Understanding
THE BLACK CHURCH

1

Who Are the People in the Pews?

Black Theology on Black Bodies . . . in Church[1]

BLACK CHURCHES ARE POPULATED with Black bodies. This rather basic claim on some level is recognized in and gives shape to studies on African American religious thought and life over the past several decades. Unfortunately within much of this scholarship Black bodies are a "shadow," or inferred (assumed) reality. That is to say, attention has been given to the consequences of living within a Black body—racism and so on. But what of the very nature and meaning of these bodies?

In this chapter I give attention to a new movement within Black and Womanist theologies meant to address the question above. I accomplish this through a turn to four recent and key texts related to the construction and presentation of Black bodies. The first two texts, by Mark Smith and Michael D. Harris, provide theoretical context, and the books by Kelly Brown Douglas and Dwight Hopkins suggest particular ways to think about these Black bodies within the context of Black churches. Ultimately, through an interrogation of these texts, I offer a way of framing a plausible understanding of who is in the church pew as a necessary precondition for any other work. It is only after this discussion that proper groundwork is in place for interrogation of the issues and concerns presented in the remaining chapters.

---

1. This chapter first appeared as a review essay of *How Race Is Made*, by Mark Smith; *Being Human*, by Dwight Hopkins; *What's Faith Got to Do with It?* by Kelly Brown Douglas; and *Colored Pictures*, by Michael D. Harris, *Religious Studies Review*, 1–8. It appears here with minor alterations. In addition, some of the ideas explored and language used here also frame the larger argument found in Pinn, "King and the Civil Rights Movement," forthcoming.

3

Constructing and "Sensing" the Raced Body

Allow me to begin this study with a simple claim that harkens back to the first several sentences of this chapter: Bodies represent contested terrain.[2] Black bodies have played this role in rather unique ways. Many who study Black churches think of this construction and deconstruction of Black bodies in terms of how they occupy economic, and political contexts as well as social time and space.[3] This posture is to be expected to the extent Black religious studies is concerned with liberative responses to socioeconomic injustice framed by an ontological understanding of Blackness harnessed to the written text with the visible as the basis of analysis and activism. To narrow the focus, this thinking is in keeping with the theological lineage of Black theology and Womanist theology, as they grow out of theological liberalism and its concern with the humanity of Christ in addition to consequential attention to the nature and substance of humans on the level of existential realities. However, current research suggests a question: Is such an approach adequate to the task? Is racial construction and racism based merely on physical vision? What of the other senses?

Mark Smith, in *How Race Is Made*,[4] suggests that slavery and segregation as basic examples of racial discrimination are not premised strictly on the observable in that the physical appearance of a slave, "Blackness" as the visual marker of servitude and inferiority, loses its force through, for example, the physical appearance of offspring of enslaved Africans and Whites. As race is a social construct, the manner in which those 'raced' bodies are marked and distinguished is also a matter of social construction—and the increasingly messy nature of discrimination required attention to more than what the eye revealed. Consequently, other human senses such as smell, touch, hearing, and taste were used to

---

2. Drawing from sociology of the body, I would suggest a useful definition involves the body as discursive construction *and* biomedical reality. Some attention is given to this here. However, I give greater explication of this in *Embodiment and the New Shape of Black Theological Thought*, to be published by New York University Press. I must note that I am not suggesting only "Blackness" or race should be of concern. As the book as a whole suggests, I understand the realities within Black churches to extend well beyond race. And my use of Womanist scholarship in this and the other chapters also points to my recognition of gender as an ongoing concern.

3. See for example Featherstone et al., *The Body*.

4. Smith, *How Race Is Made: Slavery, Segregation, and the Senses*.

distinguish categories of existential and ontological value in ways vision did not match since the eye often could be deceived. In an ironic twist, this process of "sensing" the world as a raced context was predicated on the very "privileges" of contact and control upon which the institution of slavery rested, and upon the assumed infrastructures of discrimination *qua* segregation. As Smith puts it, "people sensed their worlds—heard sounds they did not want to hear (we are without ear lids, after all), had to smell smells they did not want to smell, used the putatively premodern, proximate, nonvisual senses to invent 'modern' racial stereotypes— we begin to understand the historically conditioned, visceral, emotional aspect of racial construction and racism."[5]

In the early stages of modern race relations there was an important connection between "race-thinking and gut-feeling."[6] Smith suggests attention to race as defined beyond the visual allowed for a certain comfort with the social world as it existed in that one could associate negative sensations with "Blackness" without having to give a great deal of thought to the ramifications of this making of Black bodies.

Sensory marking of Blackness is an old enterprise, gaining its most demonic dimensions during the eighteenth and nineteenth centuries. During that period, racists pushed the inferiority of Africans based on sensory arguments that Africans had a distinctively tough skin best suited for hard work. And, furthermore, it was argued that the presence of Black bodies could be noted without appeal to vision through the overwhelmingly unpleasant smell associated with those bodies.

Blacks not only presented themselves to the senses of Whites in an unpleasant manner, but Blacks also sensed the world differently—with less refinement and without the type of reasonableness that marked the behavior and capabilities of Whites. What is more, Whites supporting the slave system suggested at times that sensory capabilities of Blacks were similar to those of various domestic animals. "Planters," Smith writes, "summoned slaves as they summoned animals. Some thought dogs and blacks understood whistles by means of sharp ears, although slaves, as humans, earned a slightly different tone than dogs."[7] Appeal to the senses also allowed a cushion against the graphic need for punishment in that,

---

5. Ibid., 3–4.

6. Ibid., 2.

7. Ibid., 22.

for example, Black skins assumed thickness and odd texture meant limited sensation. Hence, beatings were pedagogically useful but of limited pain. Such a rationale might, for a limited period at least, subordinate the visible signs of punishment such as maimed bodies and thick scar tissue on Black backs.

While there was ongoing debate concerning the religious-theological rationale for enslavement, smell, touch, taste, and hearing provided a respite of sorts for slavery sympathizers in that these senses could be used to bracket pressing demands for rationale arguments. The senses provided modalities of differentiation that did not require the hard work of thought; rather, they justified "gut-feeling." What is more, sensory perception provided rules of engagement and cartography of difference that did not require years of experience. Even small children could learn and employ the sense-based arrangement of beings. What must be remembered, however, Smith notes, is that the ability to sense the nature of this difference was also a matter of geography in that some southerners argued northerners opposed to slavery might have the same forms of sensory perceptions as southern Whites but their lack of sociocultural familiarity with the South prevented them from fully appreciating the sensory otherness of Blacks.

Whites were not alone in sensing the presence of the "other." Enslaved Africans and their descendents also marked the parameters of whiteness through more than the visual appearance of bodies. Yet Blacks could not, without reenforcing the logic of discrimination, suggest the legitimacy of "an innate sensory dimension to whiteness."[8] Rather, Blacks tended to challenge racial discrimination and identification by giving socioeconomic mandates for particular sounds and smells. For example, many Blacks argued the smell they carried on their bodies resulted *from* hard work and such smells were not inherent but were a matter of social and economic constructions beyond their control. While whiteness was also sensed, the sensual markers of this social construct were mild in comparison—even when sensing the bodies of poor Whites. Although not well dressed, smelling of hard work, and sounding unrefined, these Whites, the argument goes, did not have negative sensual indicators understood as markers of inherent inferiority. Rather, less than pleasant sensual experience of their presence was typically understood as the consequences of poverty. After all, they were not well presented, not pleasing to the ear; but they

8. Ibid., 8.

did not have Black bodies. In reviewing this sensory distinction between Black and White bodies, it is important to recognize that Blackness posed a threat, according to the stratagems of sensory perception, to all Whites regardless of their socioeconomic standing.

Sensory information was always funneled through sociopolitical considerations that meant a continuing distinction between Blackness and Whiteness regardless of what might appear to the senses as overlap. Based on sensory perception, Blackness was understood as an existential and ontological prison from which African Americans could not escape regardless of how their appearance (through light skin) might confuse the eye. By extension, gender construction took on an ephemeral quality in comparison to the heavy lifting accomplished by Black sensory difference. Hence, according to Smith, the "look" of womanhood, for instance, took a back seat to the general sensory perception of Blackness. In short, Black women were first Black and then something resembling women (when the latter served the interests of Whites).[9]

White sensory presentation painted Black bodies a site of *disease* (literal and figurative) and *dis-ease* (sociopolitical and cultural). Nevertheless, Whites ran the risk of contamination (of becoming Black) only when they acted in ways that challenged the structures of discrimination and separation. The genius of White supremacy involved the bracketing of any sustained need to recognize and address the ironic nature of this situation. In a word, "blackness would always betray itself to white senses. It had to." Smith is able to make such a strong claim in that sensory evidence was difficult to refute because it involved "subjective authority."[10]

Race as framed by the senses involved restriction of a sort; but, as Smith remarks, it was a form of limited confinement that did not prevent all interactions between Whites and racialized bodies. To the contrary, this confinement entailed a weak prophylactic against contamination in that Whites could penetrate segregation ordained by the senses at will—hearing, touching, smelling, and tasting Blackness—without grave existen-

---

9. This logic can be troubling in that a similar perspective resulted in the failure of Black liberation theology to address issues of gender during its first decade of existence. It was assumed attention to race—as the primary marker of discrimination—would help alleviate other forms of injustice. One of the challenges posed by Womanist theology involved a call for recognition of synergy between various modalities of discrimination that requires links between protest efforts.

10. Smith, *How Race Is Made*, 58.

tial risk and ontological damage. On the other hand, African Americans were hard pressed to do likewise.

With the end of slavery, the ability of African Americans to shift geography and occupy space with fewer restrictions made it difficult to "know" them in ways that fixed them within local histories and subsequent social arrangements. In response, Jim Crow regulations appealed to sensory information because the limited freedom experienced by African Americans afforded them opportunity to "learn" and "mimic" the bearing of White Americans. Following Smith's line of argumentation, landmark U.S. Supreme Court cases such as *Plessy v. Ferguson* and *Brown v. Board of Education* spoke to this shifting need for nonvisual markers of and justifications for racial separation.[11] Put differently, if one could not see an African American, one could certainly smell or feel the presence of an African American, and mechanisms were necessary to adjudicate this presence. It is not always clear in Smith's book exactly how sensory perceptions actually changed over time—from slavery to Jim Crow—to accommodate shifts in Black population and other socioeconomic factors. And while one might assume liberal theology's (and liberal religion's) humanization of Christianity might have had implications for sensory perceptions' links to religious "truths" after the period of slavery, Smith makes little of this.

What Smith presents with great insight and clarity is the manner in which race and racism are not simply a matter of thought, but also of aesthetics—a creation of the body in ways that speak to notions of beauty and the grotesque as encountered by a full range of sensors. The aesthetics of discrimination became more complex and multidimensional over time, with increasing presence in popular icons and images. Mindful of this, one might consider Smith's text in conjunction with the aesthetics of Black bodies discussed through expressive culture as highlighted in texts such as Michael D. Harris's *Colored Pictures*.[12]

---

11. Books on this case include Waldo Martin, ed., *Brown v. Board of Education*; and James T. Patterson, *Brown v. Board of Education*. I must thank Juan Floyd-Thomas for bringing to my attention Derrick Bell's work on this case: Bell, *Silent Covenants*.

12. Harris, *Colored Pictures: Race and Visual Representation*.

"Picturing" Raced Bodies

Harris speaks to the negative aesthetics of Black bodies and the manner in which African Americans constructed cultural alternatives to those images. And while this text does not concern itself with more than visual forms of representation, there remain ways in which it suggests synergy between the sensory nature of race and racism outlined by Smith and visual constructions of Blackness. For example, images of small Black children eating watermelon establish both the physical appearance of these children and their taste (i.e., foods preferred by African Americans over against the diet of Whites). Furthermore, the fact that these small children are often depicted as the prey of alligators speaks to their taste in yet another way.

From the period of slavery on, Smith and Harris point to the creative manner in which African Americans signified and twisted sensory discrimination, using their senses for the purposes of freedom and liberation. For example, use of songs (hearing?) to express subversive messages among other activities suggests the multivalent nature of sensory perception and communication.

> Didn't my Lord deliver Daniel
> Deliver Daniel, deliver Daniel
> Didn't my Lord deliver Daniel
> An' why not-a every man.

> He delivered Daniel from de lion's den
> Jonah from de belly of de whale
> An' de Hebrew chillun from de fiery furnace
> An' why not every man.[13]

Beyond hearing and the use of voice, concern on the part of some African Americans for fine clothing and meticulously cared for hair marked a subtle challenge to the sensory stereotypes encouraged by White supremacy. For example, as Shane White and Graham White remark, the traditional clothing for Sunday service representing the best a person possessed spoke to a sense of self, framed in fabric. That is to say, what African Americans were on Sunday said "in effect there was more to life than work, and that a sense of dignity and self-worth could survive the depredations of an avowedly racist society. Work clothes—nondescript

---

13. Spiritual Workshop, "Didn't My Lord Deliver Daniel," 1–8.

and uniform—tended to erase the Black body; Sunday clothing enhanced and proclaimed it."[14] In both ways, song and clothing, African Americans exposed the illogical and irrational nature of racism, bringing to the surface of public attention the visceral nature of racial discrimination. As will become clear later in this chapter, attack on the internal "logic" of racial discrimination required capturing the nation's popular imagination in ways that were visceral and easy to digest.

Shadowing thinkers such as Stuart Hall, "racial discourses," Harris remarks, "though they are discourses of power, ultimately rely on the visual in the sense that the visible body must be used by those in power to represent nonvisual realities that differentiate insiders from outsiders."[15] Such images, however, did not replace the written word as a manner of fixing Black identity in a system of inferiority. Rather, the written word and the visual image worked in concert, transfixing vision in multiple ways—all aimed at maintaining a certain construction of Blackness and Whiteness as mutually dependent identity constructions. Whereas language can be subverted and signified by African Americans, visual images are not as easily attacked in that their production is limited to a select few, a certain category of culture producers who shape the contours daily practices and perceptions. In time, these images were reenforced by the pseudosciences that claimed to replace subjective argumentation with objective, verifiable, and reasonable findings.

The inability of African Americans to enter White society in fruitful ways was presented through the image of the "foolish Coon" often referred to as "Zip Coon." Furthermore, White supremacist depiction of the properly positioned African American was visually fixed through a warped depiction of Harriet Beecher Stowe's "Uncle Tom." In both cases, the status quo was secured through a deforming of Black identity whereby African Americans were deemed inherently inferior through physical appearance (e.g., exaggerated lips, noses, slanted foreheads), attire (e.g., the clownish clothing of Zip Coon), and posture. During the second half of the nineteenth century, such visual representations of Blackness were not restricted to African American males; women were also fixed in grotesque ways through visual images. For instance, the "Auntie" figure was de-sexed and presented aesthetically, temperamentally, and physically as

---

14. White and White, *Stylin'*, 176.
15. Harris, *Colored Pictures*, 2.

best equipped to serve Whites. In contrast to this figure, the Jezebel was presented as oversexed and "positioned" for the pleasure of Whites. When taken together these images depict a paradox: repulsion and fascination with Black bodies.

Other visual presentations maintained the rightness of the status quo through the placement of Blacks in an economy of labor that glorified the assumed hierarchy of life. "Usually," Harris writes, "they naturalized a social order with Black subjects on the periphery doing menial tasks or exhibiting stereotypical behavior so as to emphasize their social and political inferiority."[16] Expressed in such works was a perception of African Americans as closer to the "natural" world than Whites, and thus more deeply controlled by natural urges and passions. This was manifest often through the presentation of the Black woman's body. Portraits such as Edouard Manet's *Olympia*, depicting a naked White woman, are given their sexual energy in large part through the presence of the Black woman (fully clothed) in the background. This is because her Black body is constructed in terms of sexuality, and an earthiness that superseded the intent of clothing to hide the body. Sexuality and Black male bodies, on the other hand, usually were not connected in that "the sexualized black male body and its mythic penis potentially represented the 'ultimate sexual experience' for white women, and, consequently, the black male image had to be eviscerated of its vitality and potency."[17]

Whether depicted in a comic pose, or in a subservient posture such as seated at the feet of a White social elite, visual images of African Americans were meant to satisfy the psychological and social needs of Whites for signs of their constructed superiority. This practice reaches perhaps the height of absurdity with the minstrel performance in which the ability to devour in a comic fashion African Americans is exaggerated in a variety of ways. African Americans are given heightened visibility through their invisibility. Yet all the while the more pronounced dimensions of White upper-class existence are open to speculation and humor. In this regard, Blackness served as a signification of certain dimensions of whiteness through an exaggeration of stereotypical Blackness. Concerning this, Harris says, "the voyeuristic fascination with black behavior and expressive culture, along with the lampooning of upper-class whites, would

---

16. Harris, *Colored Pictures*, 40.

17. Ibid., 135.

seem to confirm the idea that the one who looks holds power over the one who is looked at."[18]

Hence, Blackness becomes both a sign of inferiority and a talisman by which this effect is achieved: Blackness visually represented as social poison and antidote. Furthermore, in religious terms, through minstrel performances White actors possessed Blackness, harnessing their "soul" (i.e., their genius or essence) into a blackened body. In this way, the invisibility of whiteness is amplified, but also denied. A messy mixture of existential and ontological concerns and representations are inverted; but whether inverted or not, difference remained a visualized sign of sociobiological hierarchy. Black minstrels, however, were not simply tools in the conjurations of Whiteness. Rather, Black minstrels also used their craft as a way of subtle critique against the system of discrimination. For example, according to Harris, whereas White minstrels often concluded their performance with some type of appeal to the good old days, Black minstrels gave more attention to the human dignity of African Americans through attention to complex and equitable relationships.

These and other images played an epistemological and diabolical role by providing deep signs and symbols within a discourse of race promoting structures of reality "dependent on blackness as oppositional and inferior to whiteness and reinforcing the 'truth' of the whole discourse."[19] While powerful and easily finding their way into the daily dealings of various Americans across all walks of life, these images and the accompanying language used to fix Black bodies were not without their weak spots. They were fragile constructions relying on an elaborate and flawed arrangement of deceptions. And because of this they were open to effective attack and sustained challenge. Hence, according to Harris, visual representation became a way by which African Americans challenged stereotypical depictions and offered more humanized images of Black life. That is to say, "over time, usage alters the concepts evoked by a sign, and in time African Americans began to renovate denigrating terms to resist their implications."[20] This did not entail a change to the body as biochemical reality. In this regard Black bodies were unaltered. However, the body as a symbol of the larger social system underwent continual adjustments

---

18. Ibid., 52–53.

19. Ibid., 123.

20. Ibid., 7.

by African Americans. For instance, artists such as Joe Overstreet, Betye Saar, and Jon Onye Lockard have rethought the long standing "Aunt Jemima" imagery, giving it a revolutionary edge meant to speak from and resist against negative imagery. In their work "Aunt Jemima" does not pacify; rather, her new physical presence produces discomfort in that she is depicted as struggling against race and gender confinement.

Whereas negative images were intended to reify African Americans as both existentially and ontological inferior, counterimages by African Americans sought to keep perceptions unfixed and depicting a full range of behaviors, postures, and sentiments as representatives of the complexity and positive nature of Blackness. In other words, "the only salvation was to resist the misrepresentation by avoiding any posture resembling the images, to escape racial classification, and to form coalitions within the groping in which we found ourselves."[21] According to Harris, paintings by artists such as Henry Tanner served to humanize African Americans by depicting the inner workings of life in ways that highlighted dignity, relationships and complexity over against cartoonish depictions.[22] There is nobility and multidimensionality to the posture and activities of African Americans as depicted by Tanner flying in the face of the flat and staid images promoted in support of the status quo.[23]

There is, however, a cautionary note: albeit a means of resistance on some level, reconstruction of racial identities keeps African Americans confined to the "discourse of race."[24] Perhaps the most troubling performance of this practice involves African American use of negative signs

---

21. Ibid., 82.

22. The cost of permissions prevents me from including images in this chapter, regardless of how helpful images would have been. For those unfamiliar with work by the artists mentioned above, sites housing examples of the work include: http:// nationalhumanitiescenter.org/pds/maai3/overcome/text4/text4read/saar/saarwork .html/ as well as http://www.jononye.com.

23. Harris raises questions concerning the limited range of faces—typically very light with features that did little to challenge the "normative gaze" of White sight—examined by Archibald J. Motley Jr. And regarding this perspective, Harris, drawing from Du Bois, reflects on African Americans who have developed double consciousness whereby power differentials encourage "disdain for the physical and cultural character of Africans" resulting in a "dissonance" producing "varying degrees of self-hatred among many African Americans" (Harris, *Colored Pictures*, 171). Nonetheless, *Colored Pictures* clearly appreciates the efforts of an array of African American artists to deconstruct and reconstruct the visualization of Black identity.

24. Harris, *Colored Pictures*, 187.

and symbols as a way of subverting them. Whether one sees this work as a matter of inversion, recontextualization, or reappropriation, Harris fears the positive attention received from the art world for these efforts points to their impotency with respect to radical change.[25] In some cases the resuscitation of negative images may even point to internalization of epistemological distortions that simply reenforce a hierarchy of neglect by making it "art." Why? In short, the original intent to demean and reify as inferior is never removed in a complete fashion by subversive works. Therefore, instead of this tack, Harris encourages a countering of racist images through an appeal to "African cultural, conceptual, and historical foundations" over against a "rehearsing of African American victimization."[26] But cultural and historical foundations associated with which particular cultural areas? Which moments in African history and where? Phrased differently, what is the cartography of this African conceptual and historical "terrain"? Harris provides little that suffices as an answer to such questions.

Black (Christian) Bodies: Part I

There are ways in which African American religious studies in general, and Black and Womanist theologies in particular, have wrestled with a similar concern: the proper cultural arrangement of African American life. While this has often been framed in terms of "ontological Blackness" as shorthand for an assumed historical and cultural connection between all African Americans, such a move tends to reify African American identity and gives little explicit attention to the nature and meaning of Black bodies as houses of "Blackness."[27]

However, in recent years, increased recognition of the religious-theological backdrop for the justification of discrimination against African Americans based on sensory perception has sparked attention to the significance of the body (as both biochemical reality and social system construction) for the study of Black religion. While the centrality of the

---

25. Harris references figures such as Michael Ray Charles and Kara Walker. For examples of their work, see: http://www.pbs.org/art21/artists/charles/ and http://learn.walkerart.org/karawalker/.

26. Harris, *Colored Pictures*, 222.

27. For insightful formulations of African American identity that take on various aspects of ontological Blackness, see Anderson, *Beyond Ontological Blackness*.

body has always existed below the surface of such scholarship through a somewhat anemic appeal to embodiment as the basic paradigm of Black religious thinking, the discourse is becoming more robust and consistent. Two recent publications suggest the potential for a remapping of Black Church thought along these lines.

Dwight Hopkins, in *Being Human*, attempts to engage the theological significance of the body with a simple and straightforward question: What does it mean to be human within the context of a racist society?[28] Thinking of theological anthropology as indebted to a triadic structure of culture (labor, aesthetic, spirit), self/selves and race, Hopkins frames the problematic thusly, "Our age is one of vastly expanded human roles and possibilities, introducing new ways and forms of human endeavor . . . Yet it is also an age in which our basic humanity is contested, challenged, and jeopardized at every turn by hatreds, strife, and social systems that deal in death as often as life."[29] In keeping with his roots in the Black Church, Black theology, and community development, the task he sets for himself is the outlining of theological anthropology—a framing of the human—in ways that promote human wholeness and communally liberative agendas over against the "demonic individualism" that currently marks theological construction of the human in the U.S. context.

Playing off rhetoric of God's preferential option for the poor/oppressed vis-à-vis an "integrative approach," Hopkins argues the reconstruction of humanity within the context of those suffering most (i.e., the economic and otherwise marginalized of society) will promote a healthy sense of humanity for all. Beginning with a general treatment of theological anthropology in the "Western" theological tradition (including George Lindbeck, Rosemary Radford Ruether, James Cone, Miguel Díaz, Fumitaka Matsuoka, and George Tinker), Hopkins moves into the constructive dimensions of his project.[30] It appears the author is concerned with a complex definition of the body as was the case for the two books discussed above (i.e., "*blackness* here denotes both a sacred natural creation and complex social construction").[31] However, the manner in which

---

28. Hopkins, *Being Human*.

29. Ibid., ix.

30. Lindbeck, *The Nature of Doctrine*; Ruether, *Sexism and God-Talk*; Cone, *For My People*; Díaz, *On Being Human*; Matsuoka, *Out of Silence*; Kidwell et al., *A Native American Theology*.

31. Hopkins, *Being Human*, 8.

the body is reconstructed over and against the dehumanizing effect of racism is a bit flat in that attention to the ways in which the physical body is placed in time and space in itself also provides the reconstituting of the body as constructed symbol (as a discursive convention). It should be noted that for Hopkins this redefining of the body has moral and ethical implications: A redefining of the Black body and Black humanity must entail a different posture toward the world and more liberative (and communally derived/focused) modes of stepping through the world. In this way Hopkins's theological anthropology maintains the tendency (for good or ill) of Black theology to conflate theology and ethics. For example, beauty involves more than resemblance to the "normative gaze"; it is not "skin deep." Rather, beauty is coexistent with "moral attributes," as Hopkins remarks, and involves a certain posture toward the world and certain behavioral inclinations.

With this assessment in place, one notices Hopkins's connecting of human beauty to the most significant indicator of beauty—the divine. Hence, the human is not beautiful because he/she is without flaw; only God is without blemish. Rather, drawing on African scholarship, Hopkins remarks that human beauty entails a commitment to right thought and action—a commitment to liberation expressed in every way one moves through the world. Accordingly, human misery stems from the destruction of this linkage, and it entails a detangling of the meaning of human existence and the obligation of said existence. Framed in terms of Christology, Hopkins asserts the following: "Jesus announces his sole purpose on earth to privilege the poor—the homeless, the hungry, the thirsty, the prisoner, people enslaved by labor, the abused women, humans lorded over by the powerful, the brokenhearted, the oppressed, the stranger, those without clothing, and the lowly. By removing the systematic structures of human evil while transforming the internal demon of individualism, all of humanity can eventually live together on the same horizontal level."[32] Here is the key: community as the measure of existence, as the substance of one's humanity, allows for a push against White supremacy, and the demonic power structures supporting it. In short, "*I* am because *We* are."

We are the present form of those who have come before; and, we are obligated to live in ways befitting this legacy and in hope for the future. Such an orientation, according to Hopkins, is paradigmatic of sacred his-

---

32. Hopkins, *Being Human*, 80.

tory as outlined in scripture, whereby the teleological nature of history represents developments in relationship to the preservation of community through, for example, the Exodus and the Christ Event. This pattern of life is the "intent" of the divine plan and, by extension, the inner logic of theological anthropology. To be human is to live in accordance with this maxim: live for self by living for others, in accordance with the nature of God's presence in human history. But what of the sources for this thought? Where else are the signs of this plan present to us in human culture?

In keeping with the sources dominant in his previous writings, Hopkins highlights Black folktales for their insight into theological anthropology.[33] But by means of a hermeneutical twist, these standard resources are filtered through the insights of multiple contexts. In this way folktales are examined so as to recognize the complexities of their development (including the significance of sociogeographic location) and meaning: Africa, Europe, and the African Diaspora. From this perspective, these tales are invaluable in that they provide a snapshot of how African Americans developed and arranged their signs, symbols, language, behavior, etc., in response to the ultimate questions of life. Hopkins maintains Paul Tillich's legacy of connecting culture and religion, and frames this connection through the cultural theory of Stuart Hall.[34]

Those familiar with Hopkins's work will note in this book the subtle shift in terminology away from an aggressive Christianization of thought to the more general concern with religion as containing ultimate concern and ultimate orientation.[35] While one might assume this would suggest a change in perspective, this somewhat broader understanding of religion is often overcome by a return to christocentric thinking. The somewhat more expansive understanding of religion appears overwhelmed by a narrow definition of theology. "Non-Christian" resources, perhaps as related to various forms of ultimate orientation, seem to serve only as enhancements for theology as Christian enterprise: What does it mean for the Christian thinker to learn lessons from "the freedom emphases in the conjurer, the trickster, and the outlaw types"?[36] Folktales, when examined

---

33. See Hopkins and Cummings, *Cut Loose Your Stammering Tongue*; Hopkins, *Down, Up, and Over*; Hopkins, *Shoes That Fit Our Feet*.

34. For example, Hall, "Cultural Studies," 57–72.

35. Hopkins, *Introducing Black Theology of Liberation*, is premised on an overwhelmingly narrow and Christian framing of theological inquiry.

36. Hopkins, *Being Human*, 90.

theologically, provide a wealth of information concerning the ways in which African Americans in the midst of oppression and in conjunction with the divine presence have understood and constructed their humanity, their being. In this way, Hopkins suggests there is continuity between God's historical presence depicted in scripture (particularly the Christ Event) and the manner in which Black life is touched by the divine.

Such a connection, then, serves as the rationale for the framing of the text in Christian terms: "In a word, Christian revelation is a cultural dynamic colored by the social conditions and collective experiences of peripheral communities in the biblical witness." He continues, "theological anthropology is thus a cultural process, in which an ultimate intermingles with the penultimate (that is, the God-human connection is profoundly situated in culture and housed in the church)."[37] The Black bodies, by extension, occupying the church pews entail both the world and cosmic connection to the divine. They present aesthetic wonder and value through this connection to the divine—the *imago dei*—that is present in their "Blackness." Cognizant of this relationship, Hopkins would suggest the theologian must work to secure (in relationship to churches) the welfare of these wonderful bodies.

Black (Christian) Bodies: Part II

There are implicit notions in Hopkins's text made explicit by Kelly Brown Douglas's *What's Faith Got to Do with It?*[38] For example, under the surface of Hopkins's anthropological thinking is recognition of the negative dualism that marks much theological discourse. Consistent with the liberal theological roots of Black theology, he speaks of God's presence *in* and with humanity, but with the added disclaimer that this presence is most forceful *in* and with those who suffer most. This theological posture raises questions concerning the divine/human tension within history; and, it is amplified by Hopkins's emphasis on the Christ Event as the central metaphor and reality within progressive Black Christianity. For Hopkins, theological anthropology and Christology as both positive and negative forces in Black life do not raise questions concerning the ultimate utility of Christianity. Douglas, however, raises this very question

---

37. Hopkins, *Being Human*, 56.

38. Douglas, *What's Faith Got to Do With It? Black Bodies/Christian Souls.*

as the central concern shaping the doing of theology and the defining of its major categories. As she recounts, an encounter with a student forced the question: "'How can you, a black woman, possibly be Christian,' she asked, 'when Christianity so often contributes to your oppression as a black and as a female?'"[39]

The body constructed and deconstructed in the previous texts is once again the primary concern. As Smith and Harris argue for the challenge of negative depictions of African Americans through sensory reframing of being in ways that speak to the weight and significance of African American identity, Douglas brings to bear on this discussion the history and theological agenda of African American Christianity. In so doing, she reconstructs the Black body over against the manner in which Platonized Christianity allowed for a dualism of importance—spirit vs. body—ultimately used as religious justification for racial discrimination. That is to say, while Black theology often limits its attack to racist use of the alleged curse of Ham and a general acceptance of inequality in scripture, Douglas gives attention to the theological and institutional ramifications of such interpretations of Scripture by focusing on the dualism promoted by this form of Christianity—a "closed monotheism"—and how it lent itself to a hierarchal arrangement of beings. Combined with socioeconomic need, this arrangement of being made the demonizing of Blackness and Black bodies an easy move. In short, difference (particularly as related to the physical body) was demonized, with "Whiteness" as normative. "Christianity's theological core," Douglas remarks, "compels the need to define difference, be it the difference between Christians and non-Christians or divinity and humanity. While these expressed differences do not necessitate dualistic patterns of explication, they certainly lend themselves to such."[40]

Furthermore, Christianity's openness to human sacrifice—the crucifixion—easily lent itself to the scapegoating of undesirables.[41] Hence,

---

39. Ibid., xi.

40. Ibid., 22.

41. In conversation, Juan Floyd-Thomas provided this insightful comment on Douglas's use of Girard: "Douglas's incorporation of Rene Girard's concept might need to be teased out some more to justify what Girard calls 'the persecution narrative' of the majority—wherein the undesirable minority is seen as a threat worthy of death. This is the missing link in Douglas's assertion between scapegoating and the homicidal/genocidal urge within white Christianity."

according to Douglas, there are similarities between crucifixion and lynching. In both cases, the destruction of flesh is used to ward off chaos, to restore order, to maintain a divinely arranged hierarchy of existence. This is the basis of religious racism: "if black people are evil by nature, then to eliminate them from society—as in to execute/lynch them—is a way of exorcising evil from a particular community."[42] The equation is straightforward: if not careful, Platonized Christianity becomes the language of whiteness as well as the form of White supremacy. The theological force, the metaphysical rationales offered, resulted in African Americans in many cases acquiescing to the negative depiction of their bodies.

In this paradigm of negation, Blackness and Black bodies were associated with the passions of the flesh. This was most graphically depicted in the ways in which Black bodies were sexualized within the popular imagination. Harris's text shows the visual representations of this assumed hypersexuality. In turn, building on her analysis in *Sexuality and the Black Church*,[43] Douglas unpacks the religious genealogy of this assumption as well as its corresponding ethic of containment. According to Douglas, "the sexualization of a people serves a dual purpose in a Platonized Christian tradition. It allows for religious legitimation of their vile treatment at the same time that it compels violence against them. A sexualized people are thus virtually fodder for violent sacrifice."[44] Whereas the corrective as presented by Harris and Smith entails a reassigning of value through proper visual (and other sensory) images and presentations of Blackness and Black bodies, first Hopkins and then Douglas seek to achieve this effect by rendering the body sacred through a theological (i.e., senses mediated vis-à-vis the transcendent) turn. Douglas seeks to break a theologically contrived inferiority complex. Put in the framework of Harris's work, Christianity becomes the *form* of visual racism as art.

Douglas argues that the troubled relationship with the human body renders Platonized Christianity heretical, out of step with God's connection to human flesh as seen in the Christ Event. In her words, "the very fact of the divine incarnation insinuates a sacred respect for all human bodies in that any human body potentially serves as a vessel for divine

---

42. Douglas, *What's Faith Got to Do With It?* 123–24.
43. Douglas, *Sexuality and the Black Church: A Womanist Perspective.*
44. Douglas, *What's Faith Got to Do With It?* 67.

revelation."[45] Douglas uses Christology as a means by which to reassert the importance, value, and beauty of the Black body. It is this take on the Christian faith—the redemptive act of Christ—that frames the proper posture and function of Black churches: they are to express in word and deed the ministry of Christ in ways that redeem Black bodies by labeling these bodies "vessels for God's revelation concerning the value of human life and concomitantly the character of God's power."[46] Questions concerning the power of God are sidestepped and the Christ Event, properly understood using a hermeneutic of appropriation, is said to highlight God's appreciation for humanity through the "reclamation of it" after the crucifixion.[47]

When efforts to point out the irrational nature of racism through reason fail, one turns to a metaphysical response. Jesus *is*, therefore we *are* (beautiful). This strategy is consistent with that used by many enslaved Africans who, in the spirituals and early sermons, marked out the substance of their humanity in connection to Christ: "I know King Jesus will be mine." The Christ Event, according to both Hopkins and Douglas, empowers African Americans to reclaim their bodies as spiritually vital and materially beautiful.

Final Thoughts

Questions remain in that the ramifications of an embodied theology and the implications of a humanized Christ are barely addressed by Hopkins and Douglas. For instance, how do Black and Womanist theologies embrace the humanized Christ of liberal theology and avoid some of that tradition's more problematic dimensions?

Douglas and Hopkins share with Smith and Harris a common paradigmatic structure—the negative application of power—as the motivation and justification for negative images. While Smith and Harris point to expressive culture—the artistic rebuilding of Black bodies—in the battle against deformation, Douglas and Hopkins point to Jesus the risen Christ as the exemplar of the reconstituted body in relationship with the divine. Smith and Harris give prominence to the articulation of an existential

---

45. Ibid., 76.

46. Ibid., 100.

47. Ibid., 100.

space adequate for full personhood. Hopkins and Douglas give priority to the transcendent nature of human identity, and discuss this from the context of the Black Church tradition. In making this final move, Hopkins and Douglas raise questions concerning the body's ultimate importance when lodged firmly in human history. For both Hopkins and Douglas, the Black body seems defined by faith, as opposed to the body defining faith. Hence, what's faith got to do with it? Everything is the answer offered by both Hopkins and Douglas.

Mindful of this posture the task is clear: the Black Church and scholars concerned with Black churches (as represented by many Black and Womanist theologians) have an obligation to recognize, safeguard, and "save" these bodies from the ravages of an oppressive social system.

2

(Un)Churched

Scholars of the Black Church and
What They Are Allowed to Say

A S THE INTRODUCTION TO this volume makes clear, I am marginal to Black churches, and this positioning of myself and my work opens opportunity to explore an important question: What is the 'proper' relationship of the scholar to the Black Church? Or put differently, should a scholar who interrogates Black churches work from the "center" or the "margin"?[1] My question concerns a matter of "location," the dynamics of relationship to Black churches necessary in order to engage these institutions.[2] In this way, I hope to imply something concerning the mechanics of authenticity as connected to the work of scholars (in this case I highlight theologians) on Black churches.

A Personal Note . . . for Context

Relying on memory, as problematic as that is, I would have to confess my early and graphic lessons on marginality stemmed from the theological rhetoric and religious practices of my home denomination in general and

---

1. Some material in this chapter is drawn from: Pinn, "Like Prophets and Disciples," 79–82. I also draw some material from Pinn, "Facing Competing Claims," 87–95.

2. In this way my approach here is distinguishable from mid-twentieth-century critiques of Black churches on political grounds that saw in them little of liberative value. Mine is not a question of legitimacy for study in that I suggest critique and celebration based on an evaluation of Black churches' adherence to their articulated missions and objectives. Rather, I raise a question regarding the positioning of the scholar involved in study of Black churches.

my local church positioned at the edge of the rust belt in Buffalo, New York. Sunday morning services and Wednesday night prayer meetings often included a litany of deeds and omissions that resulted in hell—the ultimate margin as negative and marginality as punishment. Marginality implied a confining and fixing of perspectives and persons through perceived power and a discourse of normalcy. It was apparent in my early pedagogical context that it was a good idea to remain in the theological center, or at least perfect one's ability to fake it.

Some might be thinking, "Of course; it makes sense now! Yes, this is where Pinn's disdain for Black churches and all things Christian begins, with a moment of early disappointment and angst." Nothing could be further from the truth. I took away from those early lessons in margin-marginality as negative space not a dislike for the Black Church but a certain level of theological suspicion and a rigid conceptual framework. Then and now, I admire the best of the Black Church tradition and lament its shortcomings.

Marginality within my college setting and then again at the divinity school I attended shaped the contours of my intellectual engagement, and fashioned a pecking order of ideas. It, of course, was not the marginality warned by my church family back in Buffalo. There was no sustained talk of heaven and hell in these contexts of higher education. My church's conservative theology was not heralded in the halls of higher education, and its ability to fix boundaries and promote exclusion was limited in scope and reach. That is to say, my graduate studies made clear a distinction between the adherence to doctrinal agreement that marks various Black churches and appeal to critical engagement over and against adherence that mark the work of the academic study of religion. The demands and requirements of my local church did not dictate what would take place in the classroom.[3] But evidence of marginality as questionable status if not a firm negative persisted. For example, marginality as uncomfortable difference was maintained in the classroom when questions or comments not from the dominant perspective were met with polite silence before conversation returned to its natural flow and comfortable thematic structures and boundaries. "How do issues of race and gender factor into the construction and reproduction of the Academy?" Silence. "There are ways

---

3. For a more detailed discuss of this topic see Pinn, *African American Humanist Principles*, "Preface."

in which gender and racial stereotypes continue to function within even the most liberal of theological discourses." Silence.

Even so, there was complexity to marginality, multiple ways of defining and understanding it. Furthermore, there were also tools for probing it. Marginality as intellectually suspect was not without its challengers, not without vulnerable, soft spots.

Exposed to so many theological possibilities and so many viewpoints, my rather rigid perspective on marginality started to give. I began reading James Cone, Cornel West, Pauli Murray, Sharon Welch, Howard Thurman, Richard Wright, and a host of others who pointed to alternate perspectives on intellectual and ideological space and placement.[4] Unlike the description of marginality guiding my church back in Buffalo, marginality could in fact be a location of creativity.

Marginality Reconsidered

I am suggesting here the obvious: negative marginality is complex, involving a proactive control of intellectual territory by the "establishment" so to speak, *and* also a reactive safeguarding of another intellectual territory by those from whom we might expect a different posture. For example, Black theology in particular and much of Black religious studies in general betray an orientation that reinscribes and tries to fix boundaries—creating an inside/outside within the margins of intellectual life. To the degree these discourses possess any power within the academy, it is by establishing a "center," a recognized locus of correctness, comfort, and consensus. Such a posture easily results in stilted discourse that fails to grow and expand, instead involving a simple rehearsal of old ideas through the rhetoric of respect for tradition.

I am not arguing for an arrangement whereby there are no boundaries, no lines of orientation and thought. Scholars of African American religion should trouble and rethink the intellectual margin—refusing to see it as a fixed "something." In the words of bell hooks, the margin as perspective should serve as vantage point from which "to criticize the dominant racist, classist, sexist hegemony as well as to envision

---

4. Some of the influential texts include Cone, *A Black Theology of Liberation*; West, *Prophesy Deliverance!*; Murray, The Pauli Murray Papers; Welch, *A Feminist Ethic of Risk*; Thurman, *The Luminous Darkness*; and Wright, *Black Boy*.

and create a counter-hegemony," is a framing of marginality worthy of appreciation.[5]

Marginality can be a reference for complex situations of contact and exchange, entailing shifting boundaries with tension between "place" and "not-place" through a thick arrangement over a vast intellectual geography. So conceived, the margin can highlight for exploration many sociocultural twist and turns, numerous points of contact and convergence—movement between boundaries. Thus, the margin is "both process and condition" offering historically situated points of cultural continuity and cultural areas of notable difference.[6] The framework of inside/out and outside/in becomes a way of capturing the margin.[7] Here is the point of great importance: So conceived, marginality forces consideration of whether we are on the creative edge of our fields; or whether we in fact are reifying perspectives and opinion. Such a position can afford opportunity to view Black churches in ways that expose both their positive attributes and their harmful dimensions. The markers of Black churches' work on behalf of better life options in line with the best of the Gospel message should be celebrated. To forget the achievements of figures such as Maria Stewart, Henry McNeal Turner, Julia Foote, Martin Luther King Jr., and a host of others would amount to sloppy work on the part of any scholar (or student) of Black churches. Yet, there are also flaws. As Cornel West notes, "the profound insights and petty blindnesses, immeasurable depths and immobilizing faults, incalculable richness and parochial impoverishment of that complex hybrid people called Afro-Americans surface most clearly in the black church."[8] Failure to critique in the harshest terms possible the continuing discriminatory patterns found in too many

---

5. hooks, *Feminist Theory*, 15.

6. T. R. Patterson and Kelley, "Unfinished Migrations," 11.

7. In my case, marginality framed as a negative can be said to result from my identity constructed as "non-Christian." But there are other forms of identity impacting me, such as my maleness, that offer a shifting relationship to marginality within our society. Hence, marginality also says something about the construction and placement of bodies. In a word, the cultural marginality of bodies is tied to but not synonymous with intellectual marginality. This is because the body as metaphor and material is placed in both time and space in ways that are thought and felt. All too often we fail to recognize the material demands of our positioning, the way in which margins are carved through and on bodies. Isn't this why sexism and homophobia remained unchallenged and unchecked for so long within supposedly liberative frameworks? See Billson, "No Owner of Soil."

8. West, "Prophetic Christian as Organic Intellectual," 426.

Black denominations is irresponsible and amounts to a failure to fulfill the obligations of the profession.

Positions and Postures

Much of what constitutes existing and critical engagement of the Black Church resists direct confrontation with the underbelly of Black churches (i.e., paradoxes that are tragic and representative of death-dealing practices). Scholars often sample the despair of life, but surface quickly to celebrate the teleological nature of human history and the triumphs of Black churches.[9] Even when critiqued, the failings of Black churches regarding pressing issues often are assumed to be the consequence of a misapplication and misread of Black Christianity's mission. As Dale Andrew phrases it, "black theology must press beyond its conclusive indictment of black church practices and examine the conditions contributing to any hindrance or distortion of the churches' mission."[10] Shortcomings, in a Pelagian twist, are often pitched as external to the tradition, a matter of taint.[11] A very popular form of this position involves an attack on the "otherworldly" orientation of Black churches, which goes something like this: Black churches once championed the full range of needs represented in African American communities—from spiritual development to economic advancement. However, these churches have surrendered this concern for total liberation and have turned inward giving priority to individual, spiritual salvation.[12]

There has emerged, however, another way to safeguard Black churches on the point of proper orientation. Regarding notions of a deradicalized Black Church,[13] Dale Andrews argues spirituality does not amount to "otherworldliness" and that it promotes liberation. He writes, "reliance upon the spiritual resources of the tradition does not necessarily indicate

---

9. James Cone's *For My People* continues to serve as a prime example of the critical engagement I have in mind.

10. Andrews, *Practical Theology for Black Churches*, 66.

11. Examples of this approach would include Paris, *The Social Teaching of the Black Churches*, 1985; Wilmore, *Black Religion and Black Radicalism*; and Douglas, *Sexuality and the Black Church*.

12. Hopkins, "Introduction," 5.

13. Here I am referencing Gayraud Wilmore's argument in *Black Religion and Black Radicalism*.

a defeated drive for equality. Contrary to many black theologians' assertions, black churches turned to these spiritual resources in the very pur-
suit of liberation. Hampered by the lack of political and economic power,
black churches possessed few resources beyond the spiritual and moral
dimensions of their religious faith."[14] Suggesting a similar read, Dwight
Hopkins argues for proper interpretation: "Only a superficial understanding would prioritize a compensatory role as the primary purpose of the
church. What has to be grasped is that the rituals of individual healing
and celebration serve to recharge the worshipers' energy to deal with the
rigors and racism of 'a cruel, cruel world' from Monday through Saturday.
Thus the church offers an armor of endurance, perseverance, self-esteem,
and hope to allow people 'to get over' with soulful dignity and psychic
survival 'for another day's journey.'"[15]

While Hopkins offers an interpretation of church practice that highlights the activism stemming from these seemingly passive practices,
Victor Anderson offers a bit more balance by suggesting the Black Church
houses a particular range of values that are applied in both helpful and
harmful ways. Anderson argues the Black Church is a significant "creative
center of value," a location of stored meaning which produces both good
and harm. He maintains that this center—as well as that of the family—
offers great potential for the development of the "Beloved Community."[16]
For Anderson, this is not a singular reality, but rather the beloved community is here meant to capture a more general notion of communal
possibilities. Bringing this about, however, requires "creative exchange"
between the churches and other centers of value. What Anderson offers is
depiction of Black churches as thick and often paradoxical and contradic-
tory organizations. By so doing, he makes more difficult the somewhat flat
presentations of the Black Church that hinder critique and overemphasize
celebration. He never loses sight, however, of the Black Church's legacy.
"Unlike any other mediating institution of civil society and the African
American community, as a comprehensive institution," he writes, "the
black church is a center of value where the public and private commitments of all its members meet." What is more, "faithfulness to the best of
the black church tradition means that all members seek faithfully to pro-

---

14. Andrews, *Practical Theology for Black Churches*, 55.

15. Hopkins, "Introduction," 1.

16. Anderson, *Creative Exchange*, chap. 5.

mote in the public realm the civil and human rights of all . . . All members seek to be faithful sustainers of norms and values that enrich the private realm of marriage, family, and sex, even if we have disagreement on what those norms and values should be."[17] Must a scholar be a member of the Black Church in order to participate in this exchange? Anderson's return to the Black Church[18]—because "it was not enough for me [to] criticize the shortcomings of the church; I wanted to be a part of its moral and social renewal"—suggests one might need to answer this question with at least a muffled yes.[19] But does participation in this "creative exchange" really necessitate personal commitment, or at least a type of silence that allows the Black Church (and its advocates) to assume like-mindedness? At work here is compliance with Black Church orthodoxy that surfaces a form of hypocrisy in that some studying Black churches with a perspective of transformation and inclusion soften their critique in order to maintain good relations with the Black Church. (Is it a "don't tell, don't ask" platform, one that allows at least assumption of the Black Church's ontological and psychological reach and connection to African Americans?)

Some ministers and scholars insist that Black religious studies in general and Black theology in particular must be in the service of the church. The making of this argument is often premised on the assumption of both the Black churches' numerical dominance in Black communities as well as Black churches' function, according to ethicist Peter Paris, as "the custodians of the black community's most basic societal values."[20] Paris's statement speaks to the intersections of social ethics and Black churches, and the following statement by James Evans addresses the relationship of theology to the churches in a way that also collapses the mission of one into that of the other. He writes,

> It has unfortunately been the case that the work of black theologians and the work of African-American churches have often been construed as separate types of activities. It would not be an exaggeration to say that the leadership of many black congregations, large and small, and the ranks of professional black theologians have looked on one another with caution and, at times, suspicion. This has resulted in a chasm in the black religious community

17. Ibid., 162.

18. Ibid., 162–63.

19. Ibid., 163.

20. Paris, *The Social Teaching of the Black Churches*, xii.

between the theology and practice of Christian faith, leaving the
churches with a religion that appears to be no more than a cultural
performance, and the theologians with a theology that seems to
consist only of abstract concepts.[21]

Continuing along this line, Evans asks a question: "How can the
dialogue between professional Black theologians and other members of
Black churches be strengthened so that it becomes clear that black theology is rooted in the faith of the church and that the faith of the church is
given intellectual clarity and expression in black theology?"[22] In a word,
"genuine theological judgment," writes Evans, "requires a praxiological
commitment to the community of faith. Theologians cannot tell other
Christians what they should believe; rather their task is to help the community understand more clearly what they believe and to assess those
beliefs in light of the major sources of Christian revelation."[23]

While rhetorically this stance suggests a sense of communal encounter between thought and practice, it can serve to hamper the critical
distance I believe is necessary to view the workings of Black churches and
assess their successes and failures. The assumption that only those personally committed to these churches can speak with authority concerning
them is a dilemma in that this required personal allegiance can short-
circuit sustained critical engagement and, of greater consequence, it can
truncate what might be considered useful or acceptable perspectives.

I have an obligation to recognize the push for liberation as the
normative structure within Black theological discourse suggests some
sense of an obligation extending beyond a simple explication of doctrinal
structures and conceptual arrangements. Hence, while filled with internal tensions, most Black (and Womanist) theologians have softly framed
theological inquiry along the lines of a constructive theology: theological
inquiry committed to reflection on the pressing issues of our time.[24] Yet
this impulse toward a public place for theological reflection is tempered
by an undercurrent of particularity—theological reflection tied to the self-
understanding of Black churches. Theology is a "second order enterprise,"

---

21. Evans, *We Have Been Believers*, 1.

22. Ibid.

23. Ibid., 1–2.

24. For those interested in a discussion of the various modalities of theological reflection, Gordon Kaufman's slim volume remains a very useful resource: *An Essay on
Theological Method.*

as Gordon Kaufman points out. However, I fear this has meant for many that the theologian is merely "copy editor." That is, the theologian recounts the story of Black faith with limited challenges to the most sensitive content, certainly not in ways that call the fundamental nature and meaning of churches into question. I suggest the theologian should be an informed critic, not a compliant copy editor.

Is the Church Always Right?

Black theological discourse's relationship to the Black Church ebbs and flows; yet it is safe to argue by and large Black theology has spent much of its existence assuming Black Church ethos as correct and nurturing. Undergirding this posture is a desire on the part of some scholars of the Black Church to maintain connection and avoid alienation from Black churches in that the self-understanding and vocation of many theologians is intimately tied to these churches and their perspectives. As James Cone writes concerning the decline in negative critique over against celebration of the Black Church, "we did not want to alienate black theology from its base in the black church and community."[25] This type of stance shapes an economy of knowledge with respect to discussion of Black churches whereby critique connotes disloyalty. "The first thing that needs to be said," Cone writes,

> is that black theologians must never speak and write black theology as if they are not a part of black churches and are not involved in the criticisms that are made against them . . . It is our solidarity with and participation in black churches that give us the right to speak prophetically. To think that we can do black theology apart form black churches is sheer theological nonsense. And if we do not return to black churches with the intellectual humility and openness to be taught as well as to teach, then black churches should not listen to anything we say.[26]

Yet why would Cone endorse this arrangement in light of the following comment concerning the Black Church? "Seldom," he remarks, "has the black church created the context for prophetic criticism to arise from

---

25. Cone, *For My People*, 110. For additional and very useful information concerning the relationship of Black theology to Black churches see Cone and Wilmore, *Black Theology*.

26. Cone, *For My People*, 117.

within—that is, from among its own clergy and laity."[27] This paradox—theologians committed to liberation being bound to institutions hard pressed to nurture and receive "prophetic criticism"—should raise a question: Can this required insider status allow the intellectual "space" necessary for sustained engagement that is unapologetic in nature? Dale Andrews poses a similar question. "The major difficulty," he writes, "facing black theology is repositioning itself within black churches without compromising its prophetic identity. How, then, can such an endeavor proceed?"[28] Yet Andrews assumes the primacy of the Black Church context as the locus for scholarship and critique.

My question should not be understood to imply a need for all theological discourse to be positioned externally to Black churches. Instead I am suggesting recognition that scholarly discourse on Black churches must not have as its final litmus test church authority vis-à-vis church agreement with scholar's work. Contrary to my position, Evans and numerous others argue for the authenticity of theological reflection as measured relationship and allegiance to Black churches. But I wonder if such a stance does not in fact foster the assumed "gap" between the academy and the Black Church.[29]

Some argue this "gap" emerges out of a vaguely defined anti-intellectualism within churches (a privileging of spiritual prowess over "book learning") and a generally dismissive attitude within the academy that fails to fully comprehend and consider the workings of Black churches. The church slogan attached to this position has been told to many would-be scholar: "Don't go to school and lose your Jesus!" In opposition to this genealogy, I argue the idea of a gap between the academy and the Black Church is premised on faulty reasoning and wrongheaded assumptions concerning a necessary coherence between the study of Black churches and the function of Black churches. In actuality, there is no gap. The current "misunderstanding" between the academy and church is better described as tension.

---

27. Ibid., 106.

28. Andrews, *Practical Theology for Black Churches*, 51.

29. It is at times suggested that there is an actual debate concerning the proper relationship between Black theology and Black churches: with some arguing for no connection and others arguing for a strong connection. While one can speculate as to who might fit each category, it is seldom the case that proponents of the former position are referenced when this claim is made. See, for example, Cone, *For My People*, 101.

For centuries, churches have relied heavily on theology for voicing concern both inside and outside church walls, motivating congregations, unpacking religious language, and demystifying rituals. Hence it makes sense that churches would first turn their attention to theologians in the academy and raise questions concerning their allegiance to the community of faith, arguing that theologians (as a symbol of the academy) should speak with the same voice and convictions as church leaders and laity. Some acquiesce to this pressure; but to the extent Black churches do not perceive complete compliance—friction abounds. This point of view fails, however, to recognize the function of academic inquiry. Such a disconnect need not be perceived as a negative occurrence or something in need of repair. Rather, this "gap" is the natural and creative distance between two strong realities.[30]

Rethinking "Good" Work

I believe rational centralism represents a way of working through the above tension. I first presented this methodology a few years ago, and argued that it provided a means by which to study Black religion in terms of both its "form" and "content."[31] Of importance for this chapter, however, is the manner in which relational centralism gives attention to both the productive and harmful dimensions of religious life/experience. That is to say, relational centralism does not assume the scholar shares with Black churches a particular faith orientation, but instead demands that the scholar explore the benefits and shortcomings of religious perspectives and opinions through a measured realism. And this measured realism involves an understanding of religion, in this case the Black Church, as marked by the doing of great good and the perpetuation of great harm.

While the scholar might in fact affiliate with the Black Church tradition, this posture toward discourse necessitates recognition that Black churches do not have privileged information or a privileged position. To assume otherwise is wrongheaded in that it fails to recognize the religious pluralism that marks African American communities and, as a result, interrogates churches as if they exist in isolation. Emerging from this type

---

30. One might raise the question using biblical language: Is it possible to serve two masters? I suggest what has been the case too often when attempting to please both the academy and the church is a failure to provide rigorous engagement of either.

31. Pinn, *Terror and Triumph*, 195–200.

of reflection is a truncated and warped understanding of Black churches in terms of their development, function, and capacities.

Suggested here is an understanding of critical engagement as a means by which to explore the religiosity (and its nature and meaning) of African Americans in wide-ranging ways. It is not tied to any particular religious community of necessity; but rather, it is concerned with a range of questions brought to bear on a variety of orientations, without privileging any one of them. Mindful of this, I want to suggest a good marker of the academic's work as productive is not to achieve or seek agreement of the faithful. Rather, it is more useful to mark the quality of the academic's work on Black churches as productive based factors such as:

1. *deep engagement* done in recognition of the church's claims and positions;

2. *thoughtful critique and celebration* that holds churches accountable for their thought and activity based on their expressed mission and vision statement;

3. *familiarity* with the existing literature and the changing dynamics of Black churches;

4. *maintenance* of multilayered "liberation" as the proper normative stance; and

5. *recognition* of the competing faith claims making up the religious landscape of Black communities as the context for study of Black churches.

The kind of discourse I call for here requires celebration but also sustained critique and recognition of the demonic within Black churches. In part this rethinking of the scholar's task requires greater sensitivity to the merit of external critique—challenges and questions from those who do not hold the same faith commitment and theological sensibilities—as opposed to assuming the utility of only internal critique.

This approach, I believe, does not take away from the work of the scholar of African American religion, nor does it damage the importance of the Black churches that mark the religious geography of African American communities. Instead, it provides context, and I hope allows for an exchange with Black churches as one audience, one conversation partner, in line with others. What is more, it opens discussion of Black churches to a variety of figures—some with personal relationship to these churches and others without. And rather than authenticity of discourse revolving around "membership," and agreement of church leaders, we would privilege the quality of commentary in light of all available materials. In this way, study of the Black Church would not prevent recognition of the complex and layered religious landscape marking African American communities. Rather, study of Black churches as presented in this chapter would allow for more useful engagement of religious diversity and would promote greater attention to a range of religious communities, including those—like Peoples Temple—that are seldom mentioned.

3

The Parameters of the Black Church

Lessons from an Extreme Case[1]

I T IS AT TIMES the case that discussions focusing on the theoretical and methodological shape of Black religious studies point to a problematic and narrow perception of the nature and content of Black religion. Take for example Gayraud Wilmore's framing of the field:

> The comprehensive cultural and holistic character of African American religion itself militates against the epistemological split that often characterizes much of what is called Religious Studies in the prestigious White theological schools and university departments of religion. The best religious scholarship in the Black academy is, perforce, 'believing scholarship,' accepting all the risk that such a position entails. It could not be otherwise. The centuries-old struggle for Black humanity in a racist environment has not encouraged the development of a dispassionate, armchair science of religion for preparing the leadership of the Black Church in North America."[2]

This quotation gives voice to a process of Christianization whereby "African American Religious Studies refers to the investigation, analysis, and ordering of a wide variety of data related to the religions of persons of African descent for the purpose of an authenticating and enriching

---

1. An earlier form of this chapter appeared as Pinn, "Peoples Temple as Black Religion: Re-Imagining the Contours of Black Religious Studies," in *Peoples Temple and Black Religion in America*, edited by Rebecca Moore et al. (Indiana University Press, 2004) 1–27. That essay and this chapter, draw from and attempt to expand upon the theoretical framework developed in Pinn, *Terror and Triumph*.

2. Wilmore, *African American Religious Studies*, xii.

personal faith and preparing both clergy and laity for a ministry in the Black Church and community, understood in terms of competent and faithful leadership in worship, nurture, education, and corporate action in behalf of God's mission of liberation for all people."[3] This notion of the study of Black religion is further restricted by an exclusionary sense of the Black Church.

This term, "Black Church," is used to signify religious communities tied together through participation in a particular history of religious formation in the United States. And, the canon of such recognized congregations and communions is typically limited to the seven largest Black denominations (the AME Church, the AMEZ Church, the CME Church, the Church of God in Christ, the National Baptist Convention USA, the National Baptist Convention of America, and the Progressive Baptist Convention). Even when the boundaries are pushed so as to consider smaller denominations and African Americans in historically White denominations (e.g., Roman Catholics), there remains in place a bias against smaller and more theologically creative modes of religious engagement such as Peoples Temple. This is an unfortunate development in that much of what is wrong with Black religious studies in general and the study of Black churches in particular can be corrected through the theoretical challenge provided by underexplored religious traditions and communities.

In this chapter I take up the challenge to traditional Black religious studies, and to the parameters of the Black Church as area of study, engendered by critical attention to communities such as Peoples Temple with four considerations in mind: (1) the elemental nature of religious experience, or a theory of Black religion; (2) the nature of Black religious community; (3) the nature of transformation as religious quest; and (4) a religious-theological approach to the tragic. The purpose of this discussion is twofold. First, I seek to present a possible revision of Black religious studies, and related to this, I hope to provide an alternative reading of the Black Church qua Peoples Temple. Through this attention to Peoples Temple I hope to trouble reified notions of Black Christianity and also add greater complexity to the ways in which we understand Black Christianity to be presented and represented. An important ramification of this new thinking involves a much richer and nuanced understanding of the nature and shape of the Black Church.

---

3. Ibid., xii–xiii.

Through a Different Lens

Much of what has been said about Peoples Temple has entailed a response to negative constructions masked by an offensive grammar of "cults" and "sects." And while important, this conversation often misses the deep dimensions of Peoples Temple, and certainly results in limited attention to the presence of African Americans in the Temple and the significance of this presence with respect to religious aesthetics, history, and cultural sensibilities. Nonetheless, one should not be surprised in that discussions of "alternate" religions of the 1960s and 1970s typically present Black political struggle but give little attention to the larger *religious* presence of African Americans.[4] Recognition of the latter, and Archie Smith is correct on this point, demands a radical change regarding assumptions of relevance. These assumptions are important because they determine what information and approaches of study are considered pertinent and of immediate utility and benefit. A sense of relevance determines what "merits" investigation and what can be safely ignored. As C. Eric Lincoln notes regarding general trends in perception: "Despite the American tolerance of other ways of faith, the American understanding of the faiths we tolerate is negligible, and has a very low priority in the order of things Americans think they really need to know about. Religions are understood to the degree in which they resonate with personal beliefs, experiences, and commitments."[5]

Related to Lincoln's observation, much of the study of Black religion is confined to a rather static sense of "Blackness" that limits what is categorized as Black religion. For example, the presence of a White religious leader—as in the case of Peoples Temple—reduces the likelihood that this community will be explored within the standard framework of the study of Black religion. And, when it is examined within this context, it is often addressed as an oddity that does not really represent Black religious expression and experience. Such religious developments are presented in the negative as an aberration.[6] Several problems inform this type of study. One is the limited nature of the canon of Black religion

---

4. For example, Ellwood, *The Sixties Spiritual Awakening*. I also point to this omission in a review essay dealing with *Christian Responses to the New Age Movement: A Critical Assessment*, by John A. Saliba, and with Bryan Wilson and Jamie Cresswell's *New Religious Movements*, 145–50.

5. Lincoln and Mamiya, "Daddy Jones and Father Divine," 6–23.

6. I have in mind for example, Fauset, *Black Gods of the Metropolis*, 1971.

and the other is a narrow range of theoretical tools—primarily Black theology—utilized in the examination of Black religion in its current and most easily identified states.

Regarding both problems, Charles Long calls for revising the study of Black religion along the lines of its theory of religious experience, noting the problematic consequences stemming from this truncated discourse. Although issued a good number of years ago, Long's conceptual and methodological challenge has received limited attention. And so a problem remains: Black religious studies has carefully outlined its sources and given limited attention to method and theory, and it is clear that the religious content explored is limited primarily to the church—and a narrow depiction of the church at that. Its sensibilities and language do not extend beyond this realm. Its approach does not move beyond a discussion, usually apologetic in tone, of the Black Church. So conceived, Black religious studies is concerned with a rather narrow question, considering the complexity of the Black community and its religious history: What is the feeling and meaning of being Black and Christian in the United States?

A Theory of Black Religion

A great deal of our intellectual energy when it comes to Black religion has revolved around attention to institutional forms, doctrines, and rituals as its basic structures. As I have noted elsewhere, these elements are the historical "trappings" of religion, the manifestation of much deeper and more elemental reality, and are most visible and recognized with respect to the oldest Black Christian communities. That is to say, while important elements of what it means to be Black and religious, these historically situated realities—church dogma, church architecture, and so on—are not all there is to religion. In fact, they represent only religion's "shell."[7]

The elemental nature of religion has more to do with an underlying attention to meaning, an urge to make meaning. This, I believe, is what Jonathan Z. Smith has in mind in saying "what we study when we study religion is one mode of constructing worlds of meaning, worlds within which men [*sic*] find themselves and in which they choose to dwell. What we study is the passion and drama of man [sic] discovering the truth of

---

7. Pinn, *Terror and Triumph*, 157–77 (chap. 7).

what it is to be human."[8] Historical realities, historical materials are, he continues, "the framework within whose perimeters those human expressions, activities and intentionalities that we call 'religious' occur. Religion is the quest, within the bounds of the human, historical condition, for the power to manipulate and negotiate one's 'situation' so as to have 'space' in which to meaningfully dwell."[9] We move toward the central concern, the *center* of religion to use Mircea Eliade's terminology. This center, I argue, entails a quest for complex subjectivity, a wrestling with history for the development of a fuller sense of humanity as the prize, to develop a profound conviction that "one's existence matters."[10] In short, this complex subjectivity is a seeking for full humanity, a push for status as a subject of history as opposed to the racist manner in which those of African descent have been projected as objects of history. It is the quest for a better utilization of human potential and creativity. Conceived this way, religion entails a mode of experience through which we seek to keep open and in creative tension a multitude of spaces of fulfillment.

This process began for those of African descent in the "United States" during the period of slavery as Black bodies rebelled against the existential and ontological construction of Africans as subhuman. Physical space— church buildings—and written affirmations are more recent developments, emerging some time after the first one hundred years of an African presence in North America. Hence a uniquely religious experience in the context of North America begins not with verbal articulation, but with the body itself. In an ironic sense, the defining characteristics and justification for their enslavement—the body—was also the loci of their religiosity or quest for subjectivity. It is this element and its display and placement, appreciation and "protection" that marks the similarity among the various traditions housed in Black communities—the Black Church, Universal House of Prayer for All Peoples, Peoples Temple, and so on.[11]

---

8. Smith, *Map Is Not Territory*, 290.

9. Ibid., 291.

10. Ibid., 290–91.

11. The complexity and importance of various manifestations of this underlying impulse—this push for greater humanity or subjectivity—should not be measured only by numerical participation. Such measuring involves a reaction against practices that are not part of numerically significant communities and that are not representative of the major Black denominations and their "accepted" offshoots.

Scholars such as James Evans sense this underlying impulse, this quest for full humanity, but mistakenly limit its expression to the recognized Christian faith housed in the major Black denominations: "Black religion attempts to help African-American Christians to sense the world as God senses it. A second hermeneutical task of black religion is to dismantle the misinterpretations of themselves and the world that undergirds American Christianity. That is, black religion is a protest against those portrayals of African-Americans as less than human or outside the providential care of God . . . Black religion attempts to provide a self-knowledge for African-American Christians by helping them to see themselves as God sees them."[12] It is important to debunk such a false assumption—Black Christianity as the only "important" mode of Black religious experience. This much I have learned from historian of religions Charles H. Long: religion has something to do with the development of "more authentic forms of community," which entail recognition of the value and "authenticity of all persons."[13] Put another way, the system—Nation of Islam, Black Church, Voodoo, Peoples Temple, and so on—is the historically conditioned manifestation of the quest or feeling for complex subjectivity. Herein religion retains some of its early meaning to bind together, but in this case it is a nourishing and binding together of various strands of existential and ontological possibility.

Mindful of this, the Black Christian bias of Black religious studies, one gets a sense of why Peoples Temple is foreign terrain for most in Black religious studies with the exception of Lawrence Mamiya, C. Eric Lincoln, Archie Smith Jr., Muhammed Isaiah Kenyatta, and Mary Sawyer. But only Sawyer thinks about Peoples Temple as Black religion in ways that do not render it some type of odd or grotesque development. Even so, Sawyer approaches Peoples Temple as Black religion within the confines of the Black Church. While invaluable work, it holds the potential to fix one's gaze on the most visible (i.e., Christian) aspects of Black religion at the expense of deeper commonalities between Peoples Temple and other modes of Black religion that cannot be explained in terms of worship style or cultural leanings but instead deal with a shared connection to the elemental nature of religion.

---

12. Evans, *We Have Been Believers*, 23–24.

13. Long, "The Oppressive Elements in Religion and the Religions of the Oppressed," 170.

Thinking about Black Religious Community

The failures noted above and found within the limited scholarship on Peoples Temple generated within Black religious studies are tied to a wrongheaded theory of involvement, a kind of elitism or Black Church chauvinism. Archie Smith, for example, noted shortly after the tragedy of Jonestown that the psychoanalytical perspective on Jonestown and Peoples Temple suggests persons drawn to such "cults" are weak minded and dependent, without clear vision and self-consciousness because they are "in search for a surrogate parent or authority figures. In other words, the prime targets for recruitment into such movements as the Peoples Temple were the oppressed, especially poor Blacks, the lonely, dependent and insecure who welcome the message of equalitarism."[14] (It must be noted that Smith rejects the psychoanalytical perspective in that it fails to take into consideration the quest for social equality.) While I agree that the "message of equalitarism" as Smith explains it is attractive, the underlying impetus for involvement is a quest for complex subjectivity having to do with more than socioeconomic goods. Instead it revolves around a much more "substantive" concern centered on greater status as fully human within a religious community whose particular ethos—aesthetic qualities, doctrine, and relationship networks—is more attractive to some than to others. Hence, participation in Peoples Temple was not a matter of socioeconomic or psychological "flaws." It was not a matter of psychological weakness or shortcomings. Rather, it stemmed from the manner in which Peoples Temple's approach to subjectivity—full humanity—spoke to the existential condition and epistemological sensitivities of some. To think otherwise says more about the researcher's personal leanings than about the nature of Peoples Temple's community and praxis. Muhammed Kenyatta turns the psychological approach on its head by pointing out the flaws and weaknesses in the society which drove Peoples Temple members to Jonestown, and which prevented them from returning to the United States. Kenyatta goes further, however, when he claims that the members of Peoples Temple attempted to create something new. "We know that the Peoples Temple became, in part, a pilgrim church," he writes. "It set out to a frontier place in the hopes of better perfecting the practice of its faith."[15]

---

14. Smith, "An Interpretation of the Peoples Temple and Jonestown," 1. Mary R. Sawyer provides an important critique of this perspective in "'My Lord, What a Mourning': Twenty Years Since Jonestown."

15. Kenyatta, "America Was not Hard to Find," 34–42.

What I want to highlight is Kenyatta and Smith's effort to point out the deep yearning for full humanity that motivated the participation in Peoples Temple of African Americans. I find this more promising; yet, there is a problem with the manner in which Black religious studies— if Smith, and I would add C. Eric Lincoln and Lawrence Mamiya, are representative—frames the conversation. G. K. Chesterton once remarked that the United States was a "nation with the soul of the church," and in like manner, Black religious studies has all too often been a field of study "with the soul" of the Black Church.[16] *Resulting from this is an assumption that participation in Peoples Temple and other religious communities must entail, finally, not the value of these communities for their members but a shortcoming with respect to the Black Church that pushes people away.* As noted by Lincoln and Mamiya: "The proliferation of exotic white or 'international' cults attractive to Blacks may seriously threaten the historic black preference for traditional in group religious affiliation is not lost upon the more alert leadership of the Black Church."[17] I suggest the criteria for an interpretation of Peoples Temple must be altered, recognizing instead the nature of the experience within that community without the Black Church as the litmus test for authenticity of religious encounters.

Furthermore, to pinpoint for scrutiny the ethical and epistemological shortcomings of Peoples Temple's leadership and membership, as is commonly the case, challenges "recognized" modes of Black religion by begging the question of similar shortcomings in the Black Church. While Smith on the one hand notes the value of Peoples Temple, he points out its flaws in a way that raises questions concerning the possibility of similar shortcomings within more easily and commonly noted modalities of Black religion. I quote at length:

> Many black people originally responded positively to Peoples Temple because it was a movement that provided psychic support and linked it with a program of social/communal outreach . . . By breaking with the insularity and seemingly irrelevant style of traditional Black church worship, many thought they had found in the Peoples Temple a form of church involvement that spoke more directly to the issue of spiritual uplift, justice, social change and

---

16. Quoted in Ellwood, *The Sixties Spiritual Awakening*, 19.

17. Lincoln and Mamiya, "Daddy Jones and Father Divine," 9. It is interesting to note that some members of Peoples Temple also maintained membership in Black denominations.

communal empowerment. Their vision of a new social order was not wrong. It was expressive of the relational paradigm. It was a vision broader than that found in many of the black churches they left. But their vision was not enough. It lacked a self-critical dimension that would have enabled them to discern the false claims of Jim Jones towards ego deification. Black people's involvement in Peoples Temple and Jonestown is difficult to explain in light of the Black Power and Black Theology of Liberation movements and developing Black nationalism of the 1960s, and the African roots phenomenon of the 1970s. It appears as an anomaly.[18]

The "indiscretions" or "misdeeds" of Black Church leaders have not been viewed as the failings of the Black Christian tradition. Instead it is typically argued that the Black Christian tradition and its value, the people and their project are much greater then any particular leader. One need only think in terms of the numerous charges—alleged and actual—leveled against the likes of Adam Clayton Powell Jr., Martin Luther King Jr., Jesse Jackson Sr., Al Sharpton, and others in order to understand this point.

Should not this same hermeneutic of the group be utilized with respect to Jim Jones and Peoples Temple? That is to say, should Black religious studies exclude study of Peoples Temple because of the troubling development of its leadership? Is there really nothing more to Peoples Temple than Jim Jones? It could be argued that Jim Jones offered African American members something they did not receive elsewhere. Can Black religious studies really define Peoples Temple strictly in terms of its leadership? This is not to say, however, that the failures of Jim Jones (and other religious leaders) should not receive critique. The damaging and damning behaviors and practices of religious leaders should be interrogated.[19] Rather, I am suggesting scholars of Black religion need not choose between critique of religious leadership and exploration of the religious movements of which these leaders are a part. Attention to leadership does not tell us all there is to know about a given religious community. Regarding this point, I think there are invaluable lessons to be learned from Cheryl Townsend Gilkes's work on alternate modes of "authority" and the more complex ways to define religious community suggested by

---

18. Smith, "We Need to Press Forward," 3.

19. I am grateful to Juan Floyd-Thomas for pushing me on this point, and helping me clarify my thinking on this topic.

these modes of "authority."[20] In addition, outside the realm of sociology of religion, a careful read of Black theology points out the importance of thinking about liberation beyond the scope of individual personalities and what they can achieve. This appears to be the lesson learned through observation of Latin American base communities as the incubator for organic and communally derived modes of leadership premised upon a central mantra—"God's preferential option for the poor"—and the recognition that humans are fallible creatures.

In light of Smith's commentary, I ask several questions:

- Is it proper to assume participation in Peoples Temple stems from the failure of the Black Church to live out its principles?

- Is there not the possibility that African Americans participated in Peoples Temple, forged community around Peoples Temple, because of its creative approach to the development of life meaning?

- Must we think about the movement of African Americans into Peoples Temple as a negative statement about the Black Church—thereby maintaining the supremacy of traditional Black Christianity—rather than as a positive statement concerning Peoples Temple's vision for complex subjectivity?

In fairness, I think the theoretical and epistemological issues lodged in the Peoples Temple dilemma are large and deeply rooted. Perhaps there is, and I want to exercise some caution here, strong significance to the manner in which C. Eric Lincoln and Lawrence Mamiya see the connection between African American "other-ness" and "odd" religious traditions. In Lincoln's words:

> [I]t was not until a peculiar interplay of social and economic factors produced a series of exotic religious movements in the urban black ghettos of the post-World War I era that 'cult' took on its distinctive, conventional meaning. Such colorful hierophants (with equally colorful titles) as Father Divine, Daddy Grace, Honorable Elijah Muhammad, Rabbi Cherry and others caught the imagination of an America which having harbored a historic suspicion about the spiritual adequacy of black religion, was now prepared to accept the black cult as visible documentation of what had always been suspected. In consequence, alternately romanticized and ridiculed in the press, such groups . . . came to represent to most Americans

---

20. Gilkes, *If It Wasn't for the Women*, 2000.

what was meant by 'cult.' . . . Inevitably, the association of cult with
the more exotic expressions of black religion encouraged the dis-
tension of the term into a convenient appellation eventually applied
in popular usage to most, if not all organized black worship.[21]

While there is probably a great deal of truth to this—the merging
of "marginal elements" in the popular imagination—the response to it
on the part of Black religious studies is problematic. It appears Black
religious studies, following the lead of early critics such as Arthur Huff
Fauset, sought to correct for this by safeguarding and distinguishing its
prized religious institutions from marginal communities.[22]

With this in mind, Smith, Lincoln, and Mamiya, at the very least,
imply a tying of authentic Black religion to a certain strain of Black consciousness, marked by what is often referred to as "ontological blackness"
(i.e., linking inclusion in the Black community with a certain perspective
on and grasp of racial markers such as specified cultural sensibilities, social leanings, and approved relationships). Regarding this practice, Victor
Anderson wisely notes in his volume, *Beyond Ontological Blackness*, that
Black religious studies reifies Blackness and holds it as the measure of
fit with the Black religious (read Christian) tradition. Hence, Black religious studies, particularly Black and Womanist theologies, have unwit-
tingly supported forms of essentialism in ways that actually counter the
struggle for a liberated existence.[23] Think, for example, of Black theology's early, almost exclusive focus on liberation against racism from the
male perspective. This preoccupation of necessity meant little attention
given to the sexism implicitly accepted by Black male theologians and the
churches they claimed to represent. In addition to the manner in which
this essentialized sense of Blackness shapes and limits understandings of

---

21. Lincoln and Mamiya, "Daddy Jones and Father Divine," 7–8. Mary McCormick
Maaga marks the development of nontolerance at a later time. Hence, "in contemporary
religious studies I would suggest the more focused study of [new religious movements]
there is 'before Jonestown' and 'after Jonestown.' The deaths of more than nine hundred
people in a jungle commune, the vast majority of whom died by ingesting a cyanide-
laced beverage, signaled the end of an era of relative religious tolerance in America and
the beginning of a time of cynicism, paranoia, and fear about nonmainstream religions,
variously referred to as cults, sects, alternate religions or new religious movements"
(Maaga, *Hearing the Voices of Jonestown*, 1).

22. Fauset et al., *Black Gods of the Metropolis*.

23. Anderson, *Beyond Ontological Blackness*.

oppression, it also restricts the nature and scope of the Black religious community.

To be authentically Black comes to imply participation in (or at least nominal support for) the Black Church tradition as exemplified by Black-founded and -run denominations. A strong epistemological, if not onto-logical, link is thereby forged between the Black (run) Church and Black communities. To emphasize this point, I turn to a passage I have quoted often because of a continuing embrace of its assumptions regarding true Black religion as exclusively Black Church religion: "In the beginning was the black church, and the black church was with the black community, and *the black church was the black community. The black church was in the beginning with the black people; all things were made through the black church, and without the black church was not anything made that was made.* In the black church was life, and the life was the light of the black people. The black church still shines in the darkness, and the darkness has not overcome it."[24]

Efforts have been made to break free of this limited depiction of Black religious communities, and by extension the contours of what it means to be Black and religious. This, however, is not a theoretical battle that is waged once. Rather, it requires continued effort to "explode" the canon of Black religion and to problematize myopic definitions of proper religious involvements.

I am not arguing links between Peoples Temple and the Black Church tradition have no importance. Instead my concern is to look not only at the ways in which the Black Church tradition informs People Temple's theology, aesthetics, and praxis, but also to examine the man-ner in which Peoples Temple might inform Black religious studies and its assumptions regarding Black churches. On this point, serious engage-ment with Peoples Temple and the effort of scholars to think about it with respect to its "Black Church" dimension raises an interesting question: what and where is the *Black* in Black religion? This question first surfaced with respect to the presence of African Americans in the Roman Catholic Church, the United Methodist Church, as well as in other predominantly White denominations. And implied in this question was a critique of Black involvement with institutions that were not developed for and by African Americans. Bluntly stated, how could churches premised upon

---

24. Joseph Washington, "How Black is Black Religion?" 28 (italics added).

"white" religious sensibilities, with a history of questionable engagement with African Americans, help the once despised develop life meaning and orientation? What becomes evident through this line of questioning is the manner in which the "proper" loci of Black religiosity are defined in terms of numerical strength—where most Black folk are found. Nonetheless, this does not explain the reluctance of those in Black religious studies to give attention to Peoples Temple, for instance, a community that was roughly 80–90 percent African American after African Americans began to join in significant numbers during the early 1970s. This, however, is not to say the African American presence in Peoples Temple is completely lost on all scholars.

Mary Maaga and Mary Sawyer provide important insights into the ways in which the involvement of African Americans shaped Peoples Temple.[25] They do so by introducing the hermeneutical category of "Black Church" as a way of exploring and explaining the manner in which a certain constituency within Peoples Temple drew on Black Christian aesthetics, theology, and culture. Regardless of such efforts, as important as they are, it strikes me that there is much to be gained by thinking through Peoples Temple as a modality of Black religion, just as the Black Church and the Nation of Islam are modalities of Black religion. For Sawyer the question of whether Peoples Temple was a "real church" requires a yes/no response.[26] In her book, Maaga argues for Peoples Temple's structure as composed of "three groups in one." The third of these three is the "urban Black Church." While some disagree with this assessment, I believe Maaga suggests that Peoples Temple and Jonestown provided an opportunity to maintain the best elements of traditional Black Christian practice and to mix them with an aggressive concern for sociopolitical activism. This is not to say that Peoples Temple *kept* all the "best" elements of Black Christian practice. That level of certainty is impossible. Rather, I believe there is in Maaga's depiction the presence of sensibilities and leanings in Peoples Temple that made the maintenance of certain Black Christian aesthetics and practices a possibility. This is because Peoples Temple was

---

25. Other noteworthy studies seeking a related humanization of Peoples Temple include the insightful volumes by Rebecca Moore, for example: *In Defense of Peoples Temple and Other Essays*; *A Sympathetic History of Jonestown*; and *The Jonestown Letters*.

26. I am grateful for Sawyer's response (e-mail to the author on August 8, 2002) to an early version of this chapter, in which she clarified her perspective on Peoples Temple as noted in the section of the chapter corresponding to this note.

not theologically and ideologically opposed to either Black Christian aesthetics or practices. In her words: "Most of the three thousand and the majority of those who moved with Peoples Temple to Jonestown, Guyana, were yet a third type of Peoples Temple member. They were primarily black and lived in urban California, particularly San Francisco and Los Angeles. The attraction of Peoples Temple for these former and current church members was the ability to bridge the gap between the otherworldly preaching of many black spiritualist church traditions and the concrete political activism of the black power political movements."[27]

This is not to suggest that Sawyer and Maaga argue for an understanding of Peoples Temple as Black Church. Making such an interpretation of their work would be far too misleading. Instead they suggest certain segments of Peoples Temple can be related to elements of Black Church tradition, and that attention to these intersections are important components of study. I agree with Sawyer and Maaga: there were certainly Black Christians involved in Peoples Temple and Jonestown. However, I believe there are benefits also to a more general paradigm for investigation—Black religion as an elemental category that relates to the Black Church but also to all other modalities of religious expression in African American communities. Using this general paradigm raises an important question: Were all the Blacks Christian?

Corresponding to this question—Peoples Temple as challenge to theory of Black religion in addition to discussion of segments of the Peoples Temple as they might or might not relate to elements of the Black Church tradition—allows for the inclusion of a variety of sensibilities that influenced Peoples Temple, at least early in its development. This does not negate the strong Christianity sensibilities of some members. Rather, it simply places Christian sensibilities within a larger arena of religious commitments and perspectives. One should note for instance that thinking about segments of the Peoples Temple in terms of possible correlation with the Black Church tradition does not necessarily entail discussing the manner in which Jim Jones borrowed from Father Divine

---

27. Maaga, *Hearing the Voices of Jonestown*, 81. Maaga's mention of Black spiritual church traditions is interesting in that it raises a host of questions. Most important to me at this stage is the manner in which it opens the possibility of traditional African religious practices. That is to say, to the extent Black spiritual churches draw on traditions such as voodoo (some of the Black spiritual churches in New Orleans are a prime example of this), it is possible that some members of Peoples Temple were also influenced by such practices. At the very least, this possibility merits additional attention.

in thinking about the nature of community. "Like the Peace Mission," John Hall remarks, "Peoples Temple was to become an extended family that offered its communal fellowship as a shelter from the uncertain world beyond. In turn, Jones used the organization of Peoples Temple as a springboard to social action, establishing care homes for the elderly, running a free restaurant to feed the hungry, maintaining a social service center to help people," and so on.[28]

Of greater controversy and importance in light of recent studies on the Black Church is the issue of nontheism in Peoples Temple. It is on this issue some scholars of Peoples Temple stumble over the same issue of theological normalcy troubling those in the study of Black religion I critiqued earlier: Black religion may be theistic or even polytheistic but never atheistic. Such an assumption, from my vantage point, is based on selective historical memory. But when African American cultural history is viewed based on a hermeneutic of theodicy, for example, the logic of the theistic norm is proven to be faulty. From the antebellum period to the present, African Americans have maintained an important presence (albeit not as numerically significant as Black Christianity) in Humanist and atheist circles. Keep in mind, for instance, the presence of African Americans in the Communist Party during the 1920s who critiqued the idea of God and promoted a human-centered perspective on life, or workers in the civil rights struggle, such as James Foreman, who rejected God and embraced human potential. In fact, he wrote:

> It is that leap of faith which I now refuse to make. I reject the existence of God. He is not all-powerful, all-knowing, and everywhere. He is not just or unjust because he does not exist. God is a myth; churches are institutions designed to perpetuate this myth and thereby keep people in subjugation. When a people who are poor, suffering with disease and sickness, accept the fact that God has ordained for them to be this way—then they will never do anything about their human condition. In other words, the belief in a supreme being or God weakens the will of a people to change conditions themselves.[29]

Examples of this perspective abound, and many have been collected in anthologies, monographs, and articles dealing with the nature

---

28. Hall, "Peoples Temple," 305.

29. Foreman, "God Is Dead: A Question of Power," 272–73.

and meaning of African American Humanism.[30] When one considers the manner in which intellectual and more popular explorations have unearthed a Humanist tradition within African American communities, there is no reason from my perspective to assume African American members were of necessity outside the more Humanistic turns present at points in Peoples Temple's history. This is particularly true when one takes into consideration that the increase in African American converts in the early 1970s coincided with the move away from theological Christianity (while maintaining an affiliation with the Disciples of Christ) also during the 1970s. There is, I believe, something of philosophical and theological significance in this.[31]

Does this growing presence support the notion that a human-centered gospel troubles African Americans? While some argue Jim Jones may have provided competing messages—atheistic communism for some or a theistic communalism for others—and there is something to this, one should not dismiss the complexity of Black religious opinion and expression as it is manifest in both theistic and nontheistic ways.[32] It seems unlikely that African Americans would remain in Peoples Temple and Jonestown if bothered by the Humanist teachings simply because they did not want to appear to be "traitors" to Jones and the community. For some this may have been the case, but it is also plausible that for others the Humanist teachings rang true. Such a connection to a nonsupernatural orientation would not run contrary to Black religion but, as I have argued numerous times, would amount to another nontheistic trajectory or modality of Black religion. Furthermore, and outside the Humanist critique, Jones's presentation of himself as a "savior" or "messiah," while

---

30. See for other examples of this work: Allen, *African American Humanism*; Allen, *The Black Humanist Experience*; Jones, *Is God a White Racist?*; Pinn, *Varieties of African American Religious Experience*, 154–85 (chapter 4); Pinn, *Why, Lord?*; Pinn, *African American Humanist Principles*.

31. Catherine Wessinger describes this Humanist perspective as follows: "Jim Jones taught that the ultimate reality, the true God, was 'principle' or 'Divine Principle.' Principle was equated with 'love,' and love was equated with 'socialism.' Jones derided traditional Christianity as 'fly away religion,' and rejected the Bible, particularly the influential King James Version, as being written by white men to justify the subordination of women and the oppression and enslavement of people of color. According to Jones, the Bible only contained beliefs about a 'sky God' or 'buzzard God,' who was no God at all" (Wessinger, *How the Millennium Comes Violently*, 37).

32. On this point see Weightman, *Making Sense of the Jonestown Suicides*, 79–84.

strange to some, would not have meant a complete contradiction to the Black religious tradition that was familiar, I would imagine, to many who joined Peoples Temple, in that various Black leaders have made similar claims. One example is the depiction of Master Fard Muhammad within the Nation of Islam. According to the official teachings of the Nation, as expressed first by the Honorable Elijah Muhammad, Master Fard is the Great Mahdi:

> One of the main things that one must learn is to distinguish be-tween the history of Jesus two thousand years ago and the proph-ecy of Jesus 2,000 years ago, which often proves to be that of the Great Mahdi, the Restorer of the Kingdom of Peace on Earth, who came to America in 1930 under the name of Mr. W. D. Fard. Later, he'd admitted that he was Mr. Wallace Fard Muhammad, the One Whom the world has been looking for to come for the past 2,000 years. According to the Holy Qur'an's chapter and verse which we have under discussion [chapter 3:41, 42, 44, 46], the name Messiah, the meaning fits that of the Mahdi more than any other man.[33]

Such claims may appear fantastic, yet there is a notable tradition of such assertions within Black religion that would make similar claims by Jim Jones theologically plausible for some within various African Ameri-can communities.

The Nature of Transformation as Religious Quest

The notion of "movement," no doubt first derived as a category of thought from what remained of cultural and social memory related to the Middle Passage and slave auctions, has played a significant role in the language and aesthetics of Black religion, hence of Black religious studies. It was and remains a powerful signifier of transformation, of a reconstituted self and community, bound together through a shared vision.[34] In particular, "exodus" and "exile" language and imagery have functioned as powerful paradigms, serving to shape epistemologically, culturally, and histori-cally dominant understandings of Black religious development within the context of North America, and the African diaspora in more general

---

33. Muhammad, *The True History of Master Fard Muhammad*, 50.

34. I have explored the religious and theological significance of "movement" in sever-al publications. See "Introduction: The Black Labyrinth, Aesthetics, and Black Religion"; "On a Mission from God."

terms. Early Black Church theology highlights the perception of African Americans as an exilic community confined to the harsh social terrain of North America as a modern "Babylon," and numerous preachers have raised the question in countless sermons regarding the angst that marks Black life: "How can we sing the Lord's song in a strange land?" It was also understood, however, that this exile was a temporary arrangement, often a matter of theodical and providential significance perceived in terms of merited punishment for disobedience to God or refinement necessary for a great work ahead. In either case, it was understood that exile was of necessity followed by exodus into better circumstances.

For some, this exodus involved a nationalistic appeal to emigration—a movement back to Africa.[35] Entailing an often-heated debate within Black Church circles, prominent figures such as African Methodist Episcopal Church bishop Henry McNeal Turner and Presbyterian minister Alexander Crummell presented emigration as a providential exodus by which Africa would be redeemed. This theological position was in keeping with a metaphorical adaptation of Psalm 68:31: "Let bronze be brought from Egypt; let Ethiopia hasten to stretch out her hands to God." This religious nationalism is expressed in altered form by communities such as the Nation of Islam that seek to establish African Americans as a "nation within a nation," separated from Whites as Blacks—godlike beings—prepare themselves for their great destiny. Some who embraced Judaism (often combining it with African American religious aesthetics), such as the Hebrew Israelites, expressed the significance of movement or exodus through relocation to Israel.[36] Many members of Black communities, including some who might have become members of Peoples Temple, embraced the "Back-to-Africa" philosophy espoused by Marcus Garvey, the leader of the largest movement of African Americans in the history of the United States.[37]

In addition to the significance of emigration as a religious and theological expression of exodus and exile language, the study of Black

---

35. Glaude, *Exodus!* is an important text related to the religious significance of exodus language for African Americans. For additional information on the Back-to-Africa Movement, see Redkey, *Black Exodus*; and Sylvia M. Jacobs, *Black Americans and the Missionary Movement in Africa*. Interesting primary materials include Moses, *Liberian Dreams*; Redkey, *Respect Black*; and Crummell, *Destiny and Race*.

36. See Michaeli, "Another Exodus," 73–87.

37. Maaga, *Hearing the Voices of Jonestown*, 10–11.

religion often highlights the importance of movement within the context of the United States as an important religious paradigm. For example, Milton Sernett's work on the Great Migration—the mass movement of African Americans into southern and northern cities shortly after the Civil War through much of the twentieth century—details the manner in which such movement is existentially and culturally linked to major institutional, aesthetic, and doctrinal developments within Black religion.[38] When the connotations of movement are noted, one gains a better sense of the religious diversity of Black communities in that during this period of migration the Nation of Islam develops; the Church of God in Christ emerges; national Baptist conventions form; and modalities of Black Judaism spring forth. All these communities are committed to the placement of God's chosen in a better socioeconomic, political, and religious place.

Theological and doctrinal alterations partially connected to institutional transitions and developments are also noteworthy in that it is during this period that the Black Church is dominated by an "other-worldly" orientation. According to Gayraud Wilmore, this involves a shift away from a focus on a social Christianity marked by a muscular interaction with pressing socioeconomic and political issues facing Blacks to a preoccupation with a type of radical individualism expressed in terms of individual salvation over against social transformation.[39]

The civil rights movement and the involvement of Black religious communions in struggle broke this passivity. Dr. Martin Luther King Jr. makes frequent use of the language of movement to express this point. One only need think, for example, of his response to those who argued that Blacks were "moving too fast" for a sense of the argument made here. King argued that the plight of the oppressed required, and God demanded, action. Subtly pointing to the progress of Africa, to the development of the continent that figures such as Turner and Crummell had hoped for, King looks back to the United States and sees need for action defined in terms of the movement of Black bodies. I quote at length:

> The American Negro saw, in the land from which he had been snatched and thrown into slavery, a great pageant of political progress. He realized that just thirty years ago there were only three

---

38. Sernett, *Bound for the Promised Land*. I also give attention to the notion of movement in "Making a World with a Beat"; and "Keep on Keepin' On."

39. Wilmore, *Black Religion and Black Radicalism*, chapter 6.

independent nations in the whole of Africa. He knew that by 1963 more than thirty-four African nations had risen from colonial bondage. The Negro saw black statesmen voting on vital issues in the United Nations—and knew that in many cities of his own land he was not permitted to take that significant walk to the ballot box ... Witnessing the drama of Negro progress elsewhere in the world, witnessing a level of conspicuous consumption at home exceeding anything in our history, it was natural that by 1963 Negroes would rise with resolution and demand a share of governing power, and living conditions measured by American standards rather than by the standards of colonial impoverishment. *An additional and decisive fact confronted the Negro and helped to bring him out of the houses, into the street, out of the trenches and into the front lines.* This was his recognition that one hundred years had passed since emancipation, with no profound effect on his plight.[40]

From the spirituals and blues to early church leaders and the faithful of other traditions to Martin King and the present diasporic struggle for equality, Black religious studies has described and analyzed Black religion using the language of movement (most typically the metaphors of exodus and exile), and has preferred to speak about African Americans through a grammar of "chosen-ness."[41] However, this has usually been done in ways that do not problematize the liberative effects of movement. That is to say, little attention has been given to religious communities for whom the language of movement is significant but for whom it does not necessarily generate the type of praxis traditional formulations of ethics would sanction. As a result, we have missed an opportunity to enhance the theoretical framework that informs Black religious studies (and perceptions of Black Christianity in particular). I suggest Peoples Temple is a case in point.

Peoples Temple's theological framework shares with other modalities of Black religion a concern with exodus and exile as paradigms of transformation. As Maaga notes, "These were people who had internalized Marcus Garvey's Back to Africa movement during the 1920s; almost half of the elderly residents of Jonestown had already migrated once from the American South to California in search of a more just society."[42] The very movement from the United States to Jonestown marked the

---

40. King, *Why We Can't Wait*, 523 (italics added).

41. See Gomez, *Reversing Sail*.

42. Maaga, *Hearing the Voices of Jonestown*, 10–11.

continuation of flight to better circumstances. What we must remember from this is the importance of "space" for the unpacking of visions regarding social transformation. The system of ethics advocated by Peoples Temple was concerned with the creation of space in which the development of complex identity or multidimensional subjectivity could be worked out. In other words, "We are always in negotiation, not with a single set of oppositions that place us always in the same relation to others, but with a series of different positionalities. Each has for us its point of profound subjective identification."[43]

The measuring of one's commitment to this norm (a process of more liberated identity) is understood in terms of fidelity or faithfulness to the creation of this "safe" space. What Ira G. Zepp Jr. says concerning communal "ritual or ceremonial centers" is worth noting. The space in which communities such as Peoples Temple live and "have their being" is the axis mundi, the "axle or pole around which" their collective and individual identity turn "and without which [their] world would collapse."[44] Furthermore, the blind tenacity with which the "threat" to Jonestown from external forces and assumed internal "traitors" was fought speaks to the importance of this center because, again borrowing a concept from Zepp, "as humans we have a profound need to repudiate, if not escape, the disorder and brokenness of life, and to establish islands of stability as a counterpoint to chaos. The reaction of a center is usually the way people resist disorder."[45] In this space believers feel a sense of ease, of purpose and order that is defended fiercely because the structure of reality that marks Peoples Temple and other religious communities is dependent upon it for the reconstitution of socioeconomic, political, cultural, and "spiritual" being.

This is the nature of religious space and community, yet it becomes dangerous when protection of physical and metaphorical space is so consuming that it requires a compromise of the very principles that sparked its initial creation, when the welfare of the individual members of the community is sacrificed for the preservation of "space." What this involves is a failure to heed the metaphorical value of Jonathan Z. Smith's warning: "Map is not territory."[46] That is to say, the content of religious vision must

---

43. Hall, "What Is This 'Black' in Black Popular Culture?" 29–30.

44. Zepp, *The New Religious Image of Urban America*, 35.

45. Ibid., 50.

46. This is the title to his book published by the University of Chicago Press in 1993.

not be forgotten, and meaning must be gathered, not simply imposed. To simply impose meaning upon history exposes one to risk, and the tendency to engage in a warped vision of purpose that is superficial and ideological in the negative sense of the word. As Smith notes, "For a given group at a given time to choose this or that mode of interpreting their tradition is to opt for a particular way of relating themselves to their historical past and social present."[47] However, this balancing of past and present can become misguided and perverted, resulting in the forgetting of the initial motivations for the tradition. Moving back to the concepts with which I started this section, the significance and meaning of exodus is transmuted into a paranoid sense of exile in that the "Promised Land" does not deliver all that was promised. In the haunting words of Jim Jones just prior to the mass suicide and murders: "We can't go back; they won't leave us alone. They're now going back to tell more lies, which means more congressmen. And there's no way, no way we can survive."[48] The goal of peaceful existence guided by a self-determined set of standards and beliefs was not produced in a way that actually promoted the safeguarding of life. The "symbols and social structures" used to express and explain the ways that utopian visions fracture under the strain when *communitas* in its fullness is not found, and these visions lose their significance in light of persistent "evil." That which maintained the logic or epistemological cohesiveness of the community is compromised and questioned. Does not such a move at least in part speak to the failings of the Peoples Temple's vision for renewed life in Guyana?

In an odd twist, Jonestown entailed a desire to "disappear," to be left alone to live in "peace." However, near the end, it also entailed a deep paranoia over invisibility—a fear the community's successes and merit would be denied by the outside world. In other words, African Americans and others were drawn to Peoples Temple and were willing to embrace the Jonestown project because the Temple helped them attack and subdue modes of false consciousness, whether defined in terms of the demonic system of capitalism or racism.[49] Yet this community would ultimately

47. Smith, *Map Is Not Territory*, xi.

48. Printed in appendix B to Maaga, *Hearing the Voices of Jonestown*, 148.

49. I draw on Charles Long and his analysis of Friedrich Schleiermacher for my depiction of false consciousness. Long, "Interpretations of Black Religion in America," 136–38.

succumb, in a Guyanese jungle, to a new modality of false consciousness, one that would prove all too deadly.

Religious-Theological Approach to the Tragic

I am attentive to a seldom-discussed statement made by theologian James Cone, because of its importance for our understanding of truth and revelation. He says:

> When people ask me, 'How do you know that what you say is true?' my reply is: 'Ultimately, I don't know and neither does anybody else.' We are creatures of history, not divine beings. I cannot claim infinite knowledge. What I can do is to bear witness to my story, to tell it and live it, as the story grips my life and pulls me out of the nothingness into being. However, I am not imprisoned within my story. Indeed, when I understand truth as story, I am more likely to be open to other people's truth stories. As I listen to other stories, I am invited to move out of the subjectivity of my own story into another realm of thinking and acting.[50]

In light of Cone's words, Jonestown reinforces something of epistemological worth, lessons learned throughout the various moments of Black religious development: truth (i.e., the rightness of one's story) is not discovered, it is formed. It is manufactured. We should have learned this much from the religious history of the United States, in which "truthful" statements or stories concerning the inferiority of some and superiority of others were created from economic concerns and demonic theological formulations. Sad, but this is the process. As one form of Black religion, the Black Church has fought to make this not so, but it has remained the case. In addition, members of the Nation of Islam and Black Humanists have made this same effort, with similar results. Human hands forge truth for human purposes, and to fulfill human needs. There is no "Truth," just claims and assertions that hopefully serve the improvement of life options. This being the case, "truth" is revisable. Are the claims acceptable based upon the existing human condition and need? The ethical requirement is simple: Religious claims and truths should be tested in the arena of human experience, that is: how they "wear" on the human body.

What we should gather from the tragedy of November 18, 1978 (the day when the worst possibilities were realized in Jonestown), is a more

---

50. Cone, *God of the Oppressed*, 102–3.

critical understanding and interpretation of ethics of social transformation, perhaps based on a hermeneutic of creative tension, measuring the
"rightness" of actions by a synergy between individual want and group
good. Such a stance seeks to monitor the individual's perspective based
upon the cultural and historical memory of the group, providing a corrective for misguided critiques and warped practices. This type of life in/
between community is not a limitation on the self's quest for meaning,
rather it is an extension of that quest; in some respects, it is the culmina-
tion of that quest in that it brings into a healthy tension community and
the individual. With respect to accomplishing this, ethicist Sharon Welch
is correct in asserting that activity is risky and there is no method for the
production of moral vision that is free from risk.[51] There is no way, as
Jonestown teaches us, to guarantee humans will always operate in morally and ethically enriching ways, that the vision for transformation will
maintain its integrity. As many scholars have noted, Jonestown in part
expressed an effort to maintain a rigid distinction between good and evil,
with both camps—Jonestown's residents and their opponents—claiming
the former. But within such a struggle, the traditional dualism of "good"
and "evil" is unreliable and problematic. Sharp distinctions like this tend
to foster disillusionment when those assumed "good" are found guilty of
participation in "moral evil." This rather absolutist distinction between
these two—good and evil—does not allow for the recognition that all humanity is capable of both, and, what is more, is guilty of both.[52]

Catherine Wessinger and others are quite clear with respect to the
importance of community above all else advocated by Jonestown. In fact,
"the ultimate concern for the Jonestown residents was to preserve their
community. Loyalty to the collective was the primary value . . . Rebecca
Moore has argued that the members of Peoples Temple, and especially the
residents of Jonestown, were bonded together by their shared participation in the life of the community, which increasingly included participation in rituals of violence."[53] Or, as Mary Maaga notes, public meetings at
Jonestown provided community leaders opportunity to create "consensus within the community and for Jones to convey a sense of the special
importance of the enterprise in which they were engaged. Occasionally,

---

51. See Welch, *A Feminist Ethic of Risk*.

52. This is Sharon Welch's point in "Frustration and Righteous Anger Do Not a Politics Make," 27–29.

53. Wessinger, *How the Millennium Comes Violently*, 45, 47.

educational exercises were practiced in which people were asked to write about their understanding of socialist ideology and about their willingness to sacrifice for the survival of Jonestown."[54] Jonestown's final days involved a sacrifice first of "enemies" and "traitors" at a remote airstrip, but this was considered an incomplete sacrifice, unable to keep the community intact and to safeguard its vision of "apostolic socialism." As a result, there was a call for a more complete sacrifice, an act of violence through which the community regrettably would seek to preserve the vision through the sacrifice of itself.[55]

This does not mean effort should not be asserted to work for transformation, but it must be based on a creative tension as the desires of individuals are measured and corrected by the demands of community. This is, I believe, what Christine Miller attempted to impress upon Jim Jones during the last community meeting before the murders/suicides—a requirement to maintain perspective with respect to the nature of sacrifice (reflecting some elements of René Girard's discussion of the subject): "I still think, as an individual, I have a right to say what I think, what I feel. And I think we all have a right to our own destiny as individuals. And I think I have a right to choose mine, and everybody else has a right to choose theirs."[56]

Who is properly scapegoated?[57] Peoples Temple, whether in Indiana or California, relied for much of its history on the ability to locate, isolate, and name evil and evildoers. This ability, however, became diminished in a substantial way in Jonestown and even before. Lines of opposition were to some extent blurred: Enemies within the gates? Enemies at the gates? Let us extend this line of inquiry. What happens when one thinks about issues of psychological norms and the tragic through the lens of religious warriors such as Nat Turner, whose religious vision and sensibilities drew commentary similarity to the idea of "oddities" implied above? The theory of "oddities" (i.e., some leaders can be dismissed and their deeds explained away by labeling them "odd") must be approached with caution when one thinks of heroes of the Black Church such as Nat Turner, or Denmark Vesey, or Gabriel Prosser. Caution is necessary because of the

---

54. Maaga, *Hearing the Voices of Jonestown*, 8.

55. Ibid., 147–64 (appendix B).

56. Ibid., 153.

57. Girard, *Violence and the Sacred*; Girard, *Things Hidden since the Foundation of the World*.

unpredictable manner in which "inspiration" flows and the manner in which "contact" between the cosmic and the mundane is made manifest. It is, I believe, a mistake to think about involvement in religious communities or the embrace of religiously motivated ideals simply in terms of outcomes or end products. Can one fully understand the involvement of African Americans in Peoples Temple simply through attention to Jonestown "1978"? Or can one fully appreciate the religious convictions of Nat Turner by simply focusing on his death? Likewise, can the value of the Black Church be measured simply in the persistence of sexism, classism, heterosexism, and homophobia within Black churches? While outcomes have some importance, when taken alone they do not provide the best way to access the logic of involvement.

Part of the tragedy experienced after Jonestown is the forgetting of the humanity of those involved. By so doing, scholars ultimately deny those who sought complex subjectivity—a life full of meaning—the significance and scope of this quest. Clearly, attention to Peoples Temple within the study of Black religion in general and the Black Church in particular pushes in challenging ways. It forces a rethinking of the nature of tragedy, deliverance, redemption, and the existentially absurd. This rethinking entails a reconstitution of the theological meaning of and social space for transformation, and in this way it raises questions concerning the texture of *communitas* as well as general assumptions concerning the nature and "shape"—the contours and fitness—of the Black Church.

Part II

Transforming
THE BLACK CHURCH

4

Si(g)nful

Presenting the People in the Pews[1]

IN THE INTRODUCTION AND the first three chapters, I have made an effort to point out a problem of posture and perspective with respect to the study of Black churches. By so doing, I have alluded to the possibility, through marginality, of improved accountability for the scholar and a transformed and more productive Black Church. In this chapter, I rehearse the dehumanization of African Americans as a problem for Black churches and those who study Black churches. Both these churches and scholars have noted and celebrated the ways in which political activity and public protest have formed the backbone of the Black Church tradition's effort to rescue African Americans from dehumanizing circumstance. However, I suggest viewing Black churches from the margins points out another, and more consistent, manner in which Black churches have fought dehumanization.

The history of Black churches in the United States is well known and documented in numerous ways. And what marks much of this material is a concern with the manner in which Black churches, at their best, as one expression of Black religiosity, seek to maintain a creative tension between spiritual concerns and sociopolitical transformation (i.e., the "this-worldly" vs. "other-worldly" dualism). Sympathetic scholars often highlight the "this-worldly" dimension, using dramatic examples of religiopolitical revolution—the civil rights movement, community renewal

---

1. This chapter is an altered version of the essay published as "Sweaty Bodies in a Circle: Thoughts on the Subtle Dimensions of Black Religion as Protest," *Black Theology: An International Journal* 4 (2006) 11–26.

programs, and so on.[2] Nonetheless, I am skeptical of most blanket claims made concerning the effectiveness of Black churches regarding issues of social transformation. As outlined later in this book, there is just too much evidence suggesting that Black churches, in general terms, have a mixed record with respect to positive impact on the life options of African Americans. Nonetheless, while the socioeconomic and political activities of Black churches are uneven and somewhat suspect, in fairness I must admit there are subtle theological and ritualized ways in which Black churches seek to critique oppressive structures and ideologies, and these activities merit consideration. Building on chapter 1, as well as the larger argument offered in the first section as a whole, I want to explore in this chapter an example of this critique in the form of Black Church aesthetics. By aesthetics I mean modalities of creativity used to express the deep nature and meaning (the fullness of being) of African American persons.[3]

Black Bodies: Initial Encounters

During the period of slavery to the present, the challenge for the Black Christian has been to work out an approach to the Christian faith that promotes the healing of harmed humanity, and the nurturing of a sense of beauty within the context of a world that does not readily see her/his importance. In this way, the effort involved a theo-ritual counter to the manner in which oppressive forces destroy the integrity—both literally and figuratively—of the Black body.[4] This process involves a "transvaluation" of sorts, to borrow from Theophus Smith, by which Black identity and meaning are transformed in part through aesthetics.[5]

I develop this argument through a discussion of the ramifications of aesthetics found within the context of Black churches in light of one particular ritualized activity—the "shout." I begin this discussion with a few brief comments on the historical backdrop for the emergence and use of this dimension of Black Church aesthetics as a critique of the dehumanization promoted by what I shall call the economy of discipline.[6]

---

2. Examples include Billingsley, *Mighty Like a River*.

3. For additional information on my use of aesthetics see Pinn, *Terror and Triumph*; and Pinn, *Black Religion and Aesthetics*.

4. I discuss the nature and meaning of the Black body in *Terror and Triumph*.

5. Smith, *Conjuring Culture*, 124–25.

6. I am aware that Black churches have a troubled relationship to the Black body.

Upon first encountering Africans, the English often spoke of them as black, giving primary attention to their physical form and the aesthetics surrounding that form—clothing, behaviors, cultural activities, and so on.[7] Irrespective of the initial stance, the history of the slave trade makes all too clear that the "coloring" of Africans would not remain a nonjudgmental recognition of difference. In part due to economic and cultural motivations, it would grow to entail a statement concerning intrinsic worth and ontological significance. Historian Winthrop Jordan sheds light on the growing epistemological importance of Blackness when saying,

> in England perhaps more than in southern Europe, the concept of blackness was loaded with intense meaning. Long before they found that some men were black, Englishmen found in the idea of blackness a way of expressing some of their most ingrained values. No other color except white conveyed so much emotional impact . . . Black was an emotionally partisan color, the handmaid and symbol of baseness and evil, a sign of danger and repulsion . . . White and black connoted purity and filthiness, virginity and sin, virtue and baseness, beauty and ugliness . . . God and the devil.[8]

What Jordan points to is the manner in which the marking of Africans as "black" implied a certain aesthetic hierarchy, supported through theological pronouncements and religious assumptions that made ill treatment of Africans justifiable because they were ugly and of questionable intrinsic value.

As noted in chapter 1, Black bodies were considered different, aesthetically foreign; and what is more, they were without proper religious sensibilities.[9] That is to say, the lack of aesthetic importance was tied to a series of behaviors and attitudes that marked Africans as inferior in that a

---

While the "shout" points to a somewhat positive encounter with the body, there are numerous examples of a less-than-healthy relationship to the body and its functions. I address such issues elsewhere. See, for example, Pinn, *The Black Church in the Post-Civil Rights Era*; Pinn, "Embracing Nimrod's Legacy."

7. Patterson, *Rituals of Blood*.

8. Jordan, *White over Black*, 7.

9. Charles Long has wisely commented on the significance of flesh with regard to this development of what I refer to as the economy of discipline. In spite of any talk concerning souls and religious missions, Africans were their bodies in that "their experiences were rooted in the absurd meaning of their bodies, and it was for these bodies that they were regarded not only as valuable works but also as the locus of meaninglessness" (Long, *Significations*, 197).

lack of beauty was tied to a lack of ethical and moral correctness. As late as the 1830s, David B. Chesebrough notes, "it was generally held that blacks were less intelligent and more emotional than whites. They were also more sensual and superstitious, less disciplined and less orderly. One had only to look at human behavior in Africa, the original habitat of blacks, to become aware of how different in culture, values, and social mores the blacks were from whites."[10] There was a consistent assumption that Blacks had restricted subjectivity and identity. Their assumed aesthetic inferiority spoke to ontological inferiority, and this was expressed in the very business of slave trading and discriminatory practices emerging after the end of the slave trade.

Throughout the history of what becomes the United States, those of African descent were presented and represented in ways that exaggerated features, emphasized postures of servitude and so on in ways that were meant to make them unpleasing to the popular eye. A prime example of this negative aesthetic is found in the writing of Rev. Thomas Dixon, who described an African American accused of rape this way: "His thick lips were drawn upward in an ugly leer and his sinister bead-eyes gleamed like a gorilla's. A single fierce leap and the black claws clutched the air slowly as if sinking into the soft white throat."[11] One can also draw examples from the visual arts. The work of nineteenth-century painter William Sidney Mount, a member of what is referred to as the "New York School," presented Blacks as "characterized by physical appearance or stereotypical behavior that emphasized their 'otherness' rather than by a full spectrum of emotional and intellectual activities."[12]

A general philosophy of African American representation in the visual arts is present in such a way, particularly after Reconstruction, as to render Black Americans aesthetically, hence sociopolitically, questionable. In other words, "the visual arts of this period relied on conceptions of blacks as debased, dehumanized figures. The large number and variety of inherently racist images in American culture attest to a particularly American preoccupation with marginalizing black Americans by flooding the culture with an-Other Negro, a Negro who conformed to the deepest social fears and fantasies of the larger society."[13] The words of Cornel West

---

10. Chesebrough, *God Ordained This War*, 148

11. Dixon, *The Clansman*, 272.

12. McElroy, "Introduction: Race and Representation," xiii.

13. Gates, "The Face and Voice of Blackness," xxxix.

ring true: "the notion that black people are human beings is a relatively new discovery in the modern West. The idea of black equality in beauty, culture, and intellectual capacity remains problematic."[14]

The Economy of Discipline

The Black body had to be controlled and in this sense the manifestation of will by those with power in North America marks an economy of discipline reaching into every sphere of existence for the "Other"—those of African descent. The taming of Black flesh through violence and intimidation in order to secure the "consent" of the victim to his/her own victimization was the function of this economy of discipline. This economy also connotes a wider framework by which Whites sought to maintain societal order with myths of creation and meaning that made sense of the world through a mythology of Whites' aesthetic superiority. The projection of Black Americans as lacking beauty made abuse of Black bodies easier to undertake. To understand this, one need only consider the numerous stories of whippings, mutilations, and disfigurements provided by slaves and White observers alike. A former slave recounts life on the plantation of a widowed planter, making special note of the abuse she suffered: "He was a widower an' his daughter kept house for him. I nursed for her, an' one day I was playin' wid de baby. It hurt its li'l han' an' commenced to cry, an' she whirl on me, pick up a hot iron an' run it all down my arm an' han'. It took off de flesh when she done it."[15]

This same woman gives another example of abuse through which the consequences of the attempt to change aesthetic status met with violence. It was assumed her less than desirable physical features justified the abuse and, in a bizarre twist, also should have lessened the pain experienced:

> Atter awhile, marster married ag'in; but things warn't no better. I seed his wife blackin' her eyegrows wid smut one day, so I thought I'd black mine jes' for fun. I rubbed some smut on my eyegrows an' forgot to rub it off, an' she kotched me. She was powerful made an' yelled: 'You black devil, I'll show you how to mock your betters.' Den she pick up a stick of stovewood an' flails it ag'in' my head. I didn't know nothin' more 'till I come to, lyin' on de floor. I heard

---

14. West, *Prophesy Deliverance!* 47.

15. Berlin et al., *Remembering Slavery*, 10.

> de mistus say to one of de girls: "I thought her thick skull and cap
> of wool could take it better than that."[16]

Physical violence meant to control those of African descent served to re-enforce the required ugliness of their bodies.

As another dimension of the economy of discipline, the poor appearance of enslaved Africans with respect to their attire is not simply a matter of the demands of labor; I suggest it is also a matter of the aesthetically questionable state of the enslaved. They were not considered beautiful, hence undeserving of materials that would enhance their appearance. Their bodies were labeled ugly, and therefore to be hidden to whatever degree possible. It is true that Blacks often stylized themselves and arranged their appearance in ways that spoke against the dominant social story of aesthetic inferiority. But, as we are reminded by Shane White and Graham White, the Black body during the period of slavery (and after, I would argue) was a site of struggle, with the economy of discipline maintaining the upper hand with respect to the "look" of Blacks. This is because "blacks' bodies could still be branded, mutilated, penetrated by the owner, or bought and sold like any other piece of property."[17] Clothes worn or the particular hairstyle used by slaves and free Blacks at best brought into question momentarily the assumed ugliness of Black bodies. There was, then, a short-lived aesthetic dissonance that Whites worked hard to eliminate due to the implications and wide-ranging significance of beauty within the social world.

A clear distinction had to be reenforced concerning bodies of worth (i.e., White bodies) and Black bodies as lacking aesthetic quality.[18] The former is a body full of vitality and merit, and the latter is relatively empty of anything that deserves recognition as profound. It is because of this distinction, and in fact it is dependent on this distinction, that a common humanity or a shared beauty could be denied. Blacks' presentation was enhanced to increase their aesthetic appeal only when aesthetic enhancement increased the value of their flesh for the benefit of others, or when the sexual urges of Whites needed to be played out on Black bodies. Yet, it was always a pragmatic beauty, one that was based on a "social fact"

---

16. Ibid.

17. White and White, *Stylin'*, 83.

18. Chapter 1 addresses this through attention to Smith, *How Race Is Made*. See n. 4 in chapter 1 above.

of difference.[19] In other words, this did not mean certain Africans had an inherent beauty about them; rather, it meant differences, a sense of social ugliness, could be overlooked for particular purposes as long as social hierarchy remained intact. Activities associated with the economy of discipline were absorbed into the religious reasoning and social codes of the times. In this sense, the economy of discipline entailed an obligation embraced by God-fearing and social order-minded Whites. It is for this reason that Ira Berlin could remark that disciplining Blacks who "needed" it was a matter of honor and chivalry for Whites.[20] One can imagine how religious sensibilities and a certain type of theology would be useful in accomplishing this in that they allow for a denial of wrong doing under the guise of socioreligious necessity.

With respect to religiotheological sensibilities, those of African descent were despised on at least two levels: They had bodies, the seat of human desires that run contrary to the will of God; and they had Black bodies, which were the sign of a less than fully formed human nature. Disciplining the body was an act that preserved the subordination of Blacks ordained by God through the curse on Canaan (Ham), and through a certain type of decontextualized reading of biblical pronouncements of early followers of Christ such as this message found in Ephesians 6:5: "Slaves, be obedient to those who are your earthly masters, with fear and trembling, in singleness of heart, as to Christ."[21] What takes places might be described by Orlando Patterson as a moment of "projection" whereby Whites are able to deny their "moral perversity and violence" while projecting a theologically constructed and "perfect excuse for them."[22]

How is the creation of the "New World" legitimate without the creation of the African as a divinely sanctioned instrument within an elaborate economy? There was a problem, however, in that the Black body rebelled against its construction. The idea that enslaved Africans were primarily concerned with the soul and the securing of the afterlife—in any of its forms—does not provide an adequate response to the forms of rebellion utilized with great frequency on plantations. These rebellious activities are not the mark of slaves uninterested in the body and

---

19. Jordan, *White over Black*, 20.
20. Berlin et al., *Remembering Slavery*.
21. Cited in Patterson, *Rituals of Blood*, 191–92.
22. Patterson, *Rituals of Blood*, 242.

preoccupied with the soul; rather, they are of a different mindset, one concerned with identity and complexity of life here, and now.

Frantz Fanon has provided enduring insights with respect to the manner in which strong efforts have been made to render Blacks "other." One should keep in mind the young child's response to seeing Fanon—"Look! A Negro"—as well as the psychological weight of this pronouncement. As Fanon remarks,

> my body was given back to me sprawled out, distorted, recolored, clad in mourning in that white winter day. The Negro is an animal, the Negro is bad, the Negro is mean, the Negro is ugly; look, a nigger, it's cold, the nigger is shivering, the nigger is shivering because he is cold, the little boy is trembling because he is afraid of the nigger, the nigger is shivering with cold, that cold that goes through your bones, the handsome little boy is trembling because he thinks that the nigger is quivering with rage . . .[23]

But this effort to deform Black identity, Fanon suggests, has been met by counter efforts to develop consciousness that recognizes the importance and beauty of Blacks. Certainly, this is one way to interpret the following lines: "I am black: I am the incarnation of a complete fusion with the world, an intuitive understanding of the earth, an abandonment of my ego in the chart of the cosmos, and no white man, no matter how intelligent he may be, can ever understand Louis Armstrong and the music of the Congo. If I am black, it is not the result of a curse . . ."[24] This "transvaluation," in Fanon's context and in the context of African Americans as well I would argue, entails a push beyond feelings of insignificance—beyond efforts by Blacks to escape the body—to a recognition of the aesthetic significance of Blacks and Black life. In this way, Black is no longer a "flaw," a problem to be addressed; consciousness of the body is no longer simply "a negating activity."[25] The phrase "Black is beautiful" thereby is given depth of meaning and importance.

Challenging the Economy of Discipline: The Ring Shout

On some level Black religion—in this case in the form of Black churches, from its early formation through its maturation—at its best involved a

---

23. Fanon, *Black Skin, White Masks,* 113–14.

24. Ibid., 45.

25. Ibid., 60, 65, 81–82, 110–11.

signification of oppressive religious signs and symbols. The Black body constructed as ugly and impoverished was signified during church gatherings, and it was transformed into a ritual device through which the glory of God and the beauty of human movement were celebrated. Through ecstatic modes of Black worship, the Black body was rescued because it became a vessel for cosmic energy.[26]

One gets a sense of this, for example, early in the development of the Black Church in the form of ring shouts, a rhythmic movement of the body that must have resembled the sway and jerk of bodies, associated with trances and "ecstatic" behavior in traditional African religions.[27] Taking place in a "praise house" or in the slave quarters after the regular service, all obstructions to the free movement of the body, such as benches and tables, were pushed aside. Once those gathered were prepared, "the 'sperichil' [spiritual was] struck up," and participants "beg[an] first walking and by-and-by shuffling around, one after the other, in a ring. The foot is hardly taken from the floor, and the progression is mainly due to a jerking, hitching motion, which agitates the entire shouter, and soon brings out streams of perspiration. Sometimes they dance silently, sometimes as they shuffle they sing the chorus of the spiritual, and sometimes the song itself is also sung by the dancers." At times there was a band providing the music, but whichever form the musical accompaniment took, "song and dance alike are extremely energetic, and often, when a shout lasts into the middle of the night, the monotonous thud, thud of the feet prevents sleep within half a mile of the praise house."[28] A description provided by a former slave is as follows:

> An' den de black folks 'ud git off, down in de crick botton, er in a thic'et, an' sing an' shout an' pray. Don't know why, but de w'ite folks shoo' didn't like dem ring shouts de cullud folks had. De folks git in er ring an' sing an' dance, an' shout; de dance is jes' a kinder shuffle, den hit gits faster, an' faster as dey gits wa'amed up; an' dey

---

26. This is not to suggest that ecstatic behavior is limited to Blacks. To the contrary, Whites have also participated in this spirit activity. Yet I do want to make a distinction in that the assumption of personhood or humanity that Blacks were not allowed to make distinguishes the nature of this spiritual engagement, and in this way makes it a unique process for Blacks.

27. For additional information see Pitts, *Old Ship of Zion*; Raboteau, *Slave Religion*; Stuckey, *Slave Culture*.

28. Pearson, *Letters from Port Royal Written at the Time of the Civil War*, 27; quoted in Murphy, *Working the Spirit*, 148.

moans an' shouts; an' sings, an' claps, an' dance. Some ob em gits
'zausted an' dey drop out, an' de ring gits closer . . . De w'ite folks
say de ring shout make de nigger loose he haid an' dat he git all
'cited up an' be good fer nuffin' fer a week.[29]

The shout involves a creative rejection of the dominant religious
discourse and its replacement with a commitment to visibility, being, or
meaning. What takes places is a metamorphosis of sorts, through which
the despised gain a new understanding of and space within life, pushing through invisibility to a more complex form of subjectivity. It is a
movement beyond what historian of religion Charles Long refers to as
the "opaqueness of the condition" encountered by Africans as "others."[30]
In this sense it is the transformation of the despised into beings of beauty
and worth.

The ring shout was questioned and at times rejected by many early
church leaders because it reminded them of a slave past that should be
replaced through worship refinements reflecting White religious expression, such as proper hymns and thoughtful sermons. Nonetheless, these
ring shouts demonstrated the beauty and value of Black bodies, flesh that
could bring people into proper relationship with God and could channel
the spirit of God. Perhaps this is the unspoken theological underpinning
for Whites during the period of slavery claiming that the shout altered
Blacks and made them "good fer nuffin' fer a week." The understanding of
Black bodies as tools for the benefit of the status quo is momentarily bro-
ken through the power of self-recognition and transcendent importance,
as Black bodies become the vessels for interaction with the divine.

Such bodies had to be of profound value and worth, irrespective
of economic holdings and social regulations to the contrary. In essence,
they had to be aesthetically pleasing—in other words, beautiful. While
the structure of the ring shout has been lost in most cases, the emphasis
on the body as the vessel for the will and movement of God in history
continues within Pentecostal and neo-Pentecostal emphases on "dancing" in the spirit.

African American life, including its more consciously religious dimensions is defined by a process of alteration, a type of signification and
reimagining that seeks to render African Americans more human. This

---

29. Berlin et al., *Remembering Slavery*, 195–96.

30. Long, *Significations*, 177.

alteration, in this instance a theo-ritual move, involves celebration of the body and the spaces it occupies, an embrace of what oppression seeks to render despised, ugly. Hence, for instance, sweat, a mundane marker of labor often associated with Black bodies as machinery for the benefit of others might in some contexts become a way of measuring how "hard" the Holy Spirit "rides" a particular person. According to a description of the ring shout provided earlier, "the progression is mainly due to a jerking hitching motion, which agitates the shouter, and *soon brings out streams of perspiration*."[31]

Bodies Rethought: The Example of Sweat

One might more readily think of sweat, during the period of slavery for instance, falling off Black bodies as a symbol of the peculiar institution and its economic machinery. It might also be understood as a symbol of fear and constraint whenever Black presence threatened slavery's social order. After slavery it might be associated with the movement of Black bodies during the arduous Great Migration, or with the labor of these bodies when jobs could be found during the industrial period. Or, it might be associated with the result of push and pull on Black bodies protesting segregation during the civil rights movement. In other words, sweat marks the Black body as a biochemical reality meant for labor, or it might serve as a sign of Black bodies seeking to press against such boundaries. In a sense, perspiration might be said to highlight the physical form to the exclusion of other markers of consciousness and meaning.[32]

Regardless of this there was always an openness to the possibility that good work, labor that produced perspiration because of its intensity, could be interpreted as a mark of importance. That is to say, during the period of slavery, for example, labor had two possible connotations for the enslaved. On one level it involved status as a tool for the betterment of others; but on another level, even work served to promote a sense of humanity. In other words, "knowledge of agricultural practices or the secrets of a trade—whether it be the ability to plow a straight furrow,

---

31. Italics added. See n. 28 above. This material is also found in Pitts, *Old Ship of Zion*, 94.

32. Readers should keep in mind Mark Smith's depiction of the senses and the construction of Black bodies. Smith's argument also sheds light on how sweat on Black and on White bodies might elicit different responses. See chapter 1.

select the best seed, shoe a mule, weave a coverlet, or fashion a tight barrel—not only affirmed the slaves' humanity but also allowed them (at least in some matters) to surpass those who lorded over them."[33] It is this interpretation of work as mark of personhood that Black churches highlighted theologically and ritually, giving it aesthetic importance in part through the symbol of sweat associated with hard work as the vessel for the divine's encounter with human history. Perspiration becomes in some religious environments a marker of engagement in the life of the spirit, demonstrated through, for example, dancing in the spirit, preaching hard, and so on.[34]

Even those who could not appreciate the nature of this religious engagement note the energy and seriousness with which those of African descent approached this practice of shouting. According to one source, "often in the religious meetings, the visitor is caused to smile and laugh out loud, at what appears to him to be amusing, if not ridiculous. But the worshipers, *perspiring at every pore*, were never more serious."[35] *Sweat becomes a sign of intense contact between the divine and the human in spirit possession and in spreading the word of God. In this sense, sweat, a rarely loved substance, is signified and given religious importance.*

Body fluids such as sweat have their most profound and metaphorical or symbolic importance within the context of Black religion when understood for their role as markers of balance and harmony, or as religious protection. Sweat has a similar symbolic significance as a marker of transformation in space and time. That is to say, it is the mark of unity between the physical body and the divine "Other" to which the tradition is devoted.

Whereas the economy of discipline and its religious supports promote a theological anthropology that questions and restricts the expression of humanity on the part of socioeconomically and politioculturally

---

33. Berlin et al., *Remembering Slavery*, 72–73.

34. I understand that geography can account for the production of sweat. For example, the heat associated with Houston during the summer will produce perspiration that has little to do with the spiritual importance of the body. There remains, however, a difference in the "work" producing sweat during worship and the general labor of the body. In the same way, for example, notions of sanctification and the indwelling of the Holy Spirit through speaking in tongues does not function as a significant theological category in all Black churches; body fluids remain a useful tool in that there is no need for theological/ritual symbols to function in all locations.

35. Pitts, *Old Ship of Zion*, 38–39 (italics added).

"others," a categorization given metaphysical significance through religiotheological discourse, Black Church aesthetics has suggested a theological anthropology that involves the full humanity of Blacks and their status in connection to the divine. By extension, the transformation of the body—the humanization of the Black body—is in some sense transcendence in that the Black person through the body becomes more than is allowed or understandable based on pressing social realities, institutions, and codes.

Si(g)ns

Even substances that ooze from the body, such as sweat, take on deep meaning and importance. This aesthetic shift marks the acknowledgement of the misinterpretation that had, up to that point, defined the nature and meaning of Black being and of the dominant reaction to the Black physical form. A recognition of beauty gives deeper meaning to the one who has been "other-ed" in that it points to the inner workings of identification: Beauty recognizes beauty.

What I have presented here involves an aesthetics premised on a "si(g)n" (a sin/sign)—here understood as an action that offends the sensibilities of the dominant group through the rejection of the dominant religious discourse supporting the infrastructure of the economy of discipline and its dehumanization business, and the promotion of alternate signs marking Black humanity.[36] What we have here is my effort to put a Black theological twist on Fanon's statement: "Sin is Negro as virtue is white."[37] It is through my reading of Fanon's statement in light of the effort of Black religion to increase complex subjectivity that I define the efforts of the Black churches as si(g)n, a signifying of notions of sin meant to restrict the meaning of life, Black bodies, and Black life. This si(g)n involves the necessarily irreverent (perhaps even transgressive) behavior of Black religion when working for sociotheological transformation, or what we in Black theology have typically defined as liberation. Such a theological perspective could not be taken from Scriptures read literally or using the hermeneutic of control promoted by the economy of discipline. The enslaved and free Africans in North America recognized this, and they

---

36. I draw from Portmann, *In Defense of Sin*, 3, for this general understanding of sin.
37. Fanon, *Black Skin, White Masks*, 139.

applied another hermeneutic, another worldview to the use of Scripture. Theophus Smith refers to this arrangement as "conjure," whereby Scripture (and I would add church doctrine, theology, and rituals) is "worked" in unusual and heterodox ways.[38] Time and space are rearranged in ways that put the despised in contact with biblical figures, creating connections and synergies that made the maintenance of the contemporary social order and its underpinning untenable.

Why talk of sin, and in particular why talk of this attempt to reconfigure Black bodies as meaningful in terms of si(g)n? Aren't there ways in which this appropriation of traditional language serves to further entrench the "other-ed" within the framework of the enterprise they seek to escape? Does this use of the traditional language of theological discourse—"sin"—a language used frequently to dehumanize Blacks entail resistance or just a deep recognition of the unavoidability of other-ing? I use the term *sin* here as a way of challenging constructive theologies (e.g., liberation theologies) to give serious consideration to the nature and value of inherited theological language.

The "ground" between the colonizer and the colonized, the dominant and the "other," within various contexts is far from solid. There is play between these poles of existence, and the language used to describe them, for good or ill, is mutually dependent but used to accomplish different ends. Hence it should come as no surprise that the children of Africa in North America would use the religious language of the dominant group but subvert it to accomplish a different purpose. Deconstruct the "master's house" with the "master's tools"? Perhaps.

There are also ways in which this signified use of traditional language such as si(g)n serves to create a space for altered consciousness, for the emergence of a new aesthetic—a postcontact aesthetic of sorts. In this sense the use of "sin" as it is defined here is not simply a matter of theological aping. Keep in mind how the Black body was traditionally associated with sin. According to Orlando Patterson, "the Afro-American slave or ex-slave was the perfect symbol of sin in two critical senses. First, in his slaveness he represented enslavement to the flesh and to sin. But to the social meaning of his slave status the Afro-American victim added the body symbolism of his 'blackness,' which brings us to the second symbolic function of the Afro-American in postbellum Southern culture . . .

---

38. Smith, *Conjuring Culture.*

It provided that he was a descendent of Ham; it confirmed the concept of degeneration from pristine whiteness."[39] And as Mary Douglas notes, social constraints require attention to "symbols of bodily control" as well as a language and grammar supporting and justifying these constraints.[40] When Black bodies were defined in terms of social and religious sin, social constraints were preserved because Black bodies became a symbol of both the content and form of disorder. And a people defined as sinful could certainly not have a positive relationship with the divine, who detests sin. In accordance with much of what passed as theology during the period of slavery and beyond, it was understood that sin brought death.[41] But, as Orlando Patterson notes, this does not require physical death. Rather, it could entail, as it did for the African, social death vis-à-vis subjugation—a surrender of will and self-consciousness in exchange for restricted but continued physical existence. This is an odd coding of Black bodies in that the baring of this "stain" by Blacks did not result in the removal of guilt on the part of Whites. It merely covered their guilt with an illusion of justified abuse. This theological exercise initiated by Whites left them trapped in their Whiteness. It is an act of sacrifice, but one that hides or covers the economy of discipline in a fog of divine right, social need, and aesthetic balance.

The si(g)n of Black churches as I present it here is an act of critique, turning traditional sensibilities on their head in ways that seek to counter the twisting of the psyche caused by dehumanizing circumstances through the forging of a new self deemed beautiful. It is a countertheology that highlights a new theological anthropology with all its ramifications; and it does this through an aesthetic turn. This challenging of established mores is not new, not limited to African "others." Yet I hope it is clear that I am pointing to a more substantive reality than the idea that the nature of sin changes within different social settings.

What distinguishes an act as "si(g)n" presented here is the location of the sinner, the status of the sinner, the blackness of the sinner. For the keepers of social order this si(g)n is dangerous if not deadly in that it rends the social fabric that gives life meaning and that justifies existing social arrangements while safeguarding the comfort of those in control.

---

39. Patterson, *Rituals of Blood*, 210–11.

40. Douglas, *Natural Symbols*, xxxv.

41. Mathews, "The Southern Rite of Human Sacrifice Part II," 4.

Such a process entails a sophisticated movement, a signifying of the moral and ethical codes embedded in the warped religious discourse presented to slaves and other "others." It is an act that works against the status quo by bringing into question the discourses of power and the "authorities"—visible and invisible—that supports it. This si(g)n denies those who maintain the status quo the right to shape the language and grammar of proper living. It is a push toward completeness—toward full humanity, or complex subjectivity.

From the perspective of those who control the economy of discipline it is a sinful act in the traditional sense, but for those seeking to break free, it is a necessary push toward *being*, a necessary disruption of existing socioreligious sensibilities (i.e., the bedrock of their invisibility). As Theophus Smith demonstrates in his work on African American cultural conjuring, aesthetics within the context of Black life involves a switching or a signifying of established meanings. In other words, "at the most generalized level of cultural performance (whether oral or musical, literary, dramatic, or ritual), cultural forms identified as Afro-American or 'black' have been variously correlated with polarized forms identified as Euro-American or 'white.'"[42] A reversal of perspectives and opinions takes place in that what is called sin is a sacred act of humanization and that which was considered righteous (i.e., the status quo) is recognized for its demonic nature. The once despised proclaim their worth, their visibility and meaning. Ultimately, what Black Church aesthetics at its best expresses in various modalities is a simple reality: the assertion of subjectivity in the face of a death-dealing economy of discipline is indeed beautifully *si(g)nful*.

---

42. Smith, *Conjuring Culture*, 112–13.

5

Mishaps and Wrong Turns . . .
but Always in Your Best Interest

Theodicy Reconsidered[1]

O VER THIRTY YEARS AGO William R. Jones raised questions concerning the fundamental elements of African American Christianity's response to moral evil in the form of theodicy. His book *Is God a White Racist?* worked through the doctrine of God and theological anthropology that dominated African American Christian thought for centuries. Some, most notably James Cone, consistent with the assumed nature of Black Church scholarship outlined in chapter 2, offered a response meant to safeguard the integrity of the faith claims held by African American Christians.

The most common strategy of response involved a rejection of Jones's authority to raise his critique as opposed to efforts to think through African American Christian theological assumptions and religious structures in light of Jones's challenge. Cone suggests that Jones's critique has limited power in that it is an external critique, one failing to appreciate the foundational claims of African American Christianity grounded in the Christ Event. "Whatever else," Cone argues, "may be said about the

---

1. In addition to the article from *Theology Today* listed in the acknowledgements, this chapter also includes a small amount of material related to the work of Kelly Brown Douglas first discussed in a review essay that appeared in *Religious Studies Review* 33 (2007) 1–8, on *How Race Is Made*, by Mark Smith; *Being Human*, by Dwight Hopkins; *What's Faith Got to Do With It?* by Kelly Brown Douglas; and *Colored Pictures*, by Michael D. Harris. Finally, this chapter borrows from as well as extends my thinking found in "William R. Jones and Religiously Justified Conduct: Personal Reflections," forthcoming in *Religious Humanism*.

philosophical difficulties that the problem of evil poses, whether in the traditional definition of classical philosophy or in Albert Camus's humanism or even in the more recent black humanism of William Jones, faith arising out of the cross and resurrection of Jesus renders their questions ('Is God evil?' or 'Is God a white racist?') absurd from the biblical point of view." Cone continues, "the absurdity of the question is derived from the fact that its origin ignores the very foundation of biblical faith itself, that is, God becoming the Suffering Servant in Christ in order that we might be liberated from injustice and pain."[2] Jesus is the answer, according to Cone. The Christ Event is God's best response to moral evil—then and now.

In addition to Cone, others in Black theology have referenced Jones, described his argument and attempted to counter it also through an appeal to the Christ Event, and the implicit value of suffering as struggle modeled by Christ. Clear after even a cursory read of these authors is the consistency of their thought with the trajectory first outlined by James Cone. This makes sense in that a good number of those who either explicitly or implicitly reference Jones were trained by Cone.[3] A departure from this mechanics of response (but a modest continuation of suffering as beneficial argument) is Victor Anderson's recent essay titled "Faith on Earth: A Defense of Redemptive Suffering," a chapter in his book *Creative Exchange*.[4] He argues that much work on redemptive suffering has been presented as a theological doctrine, but that is not the best way to understand it. Rather, he wants to understand redemptive suffering as an ethical issue. Anderson defends the symbol of redemptive suffering by highlighting "the 'responsibilitist' modality of redemptive suffering in which in and through such suffering there is an exchange of powers, capacities of worth and value that issue in faith, hope, and love, not because of evil and suffering but as copresent in suffering."[5] In developing this argument Anderson does not respond directly to Jones, but rather tackles related arguments offered by Delores Williams as well as my earlier efforts on the subject. The former offers in *Sisters in the Wilderness* a brilliant interrogation of atonement, and my *Why, Lord?* attempts to extend the Humanist possibilities of William Jones's groundbreaking study.[6]

---

2. Cone, *God of the Oppressed*, 176.

3. See, for example, Hopkins, *Introducing Black Theology of Liberation*.

4. Anderson, *Creative Exchange*, 80–110.

5. Ibid., 108.

6. Williams, *Sisters in the Wilderness*; Pinn, *Why, Lord?*

Whether one speaks of James Cone or Victor Anderson, current interrogation of the dilemma noted in the work of Jones is grounded in some type of personal allegiance to the Christian faith that allows assumptions of insider status. This is fine, and has resulted in vital discussion of the problem of moral evil. Yet it has also meant limited room for exploring alternate possibilities.[7] I continue to think this issue is an important point of debate that should receive attention within Black Church circles. And building on earlier chapters (particularly chapter 1) what I offer here is reflection on this problem. My discussion takes the form of a thought experiment by means of which I work through synergy between Black Church thought, particularly one of its towering figures of the twentieth century Martin Luther King Jr., and Humanist sensibilities. In this way, I hope to offer the Black Church a way of engaging Jones rather than avoiding him.

Initial Formulations

This undertaking for me is twofold: reexamination of my early perspective on the issue of God and moral evil as well as explication of particular dimensions of King's theological purview. Put in the form of a question: What might we say about moral evil and the divine if King's theology and Humanism are brought together? While wrestling with this question, I shall give attention to four thematic concerns: (1) "Somebodyness"; (2) King and the Personal God; (3) Reenvisioning the divine; and (4) divine mishaps and detours.

At its core this chapter is heuristic in nature, involving speculation on the potential for synergy between King's thought—his personalist doctrine of God and concern for embodiment as marker of progress—and less marginal elements of my Humanist sensibilities such as a robust anthropology and hermeneutic of life.[8] For some this will involve at least

---

7. I was not prepared for the response to my wrestling with moral evil in *Why, Lord?* and subsequent work. I assumed conversations would take place—exchange and debate between Humanists and Christians of various levels of commitment. I do understand however, that for some my rather strong and polemical take on theistic orientations stifled conversation. They did not want to discuss the issue with someone with what Cone might consider an external critique in place—particularly someone who had once been a minister in the very tradition he now critiqued. I want to be sensitive to this, while maintaining the integrity of the Humanist perspective.

8. Particularly as presented in Pinn, *African American Humanist Principles*.

a seemingly odd combination to be sure, yet these perspectives are in fact connected already.

The basic principles of King's Personalism and the basic assumptions of my Humanism are lodged firmly within a larger and contiguous tradition of African American religious thought. Hence, they share an intellectual context and neither is an imposition over against the religious leanings of African Americans. Furthermore, on a fundamental level they resonate with a general ethical framework marking African American religious thought in that they both maintain something of a social consciousness—recognition that life lived must involve a push for greater options and integrity, whether one calls this push "freedom" or "liberation" is of little consequence. In a word, although appealing to different segments of a complex African American community, both are organic and reflect a passionate commitment to social transformation and communal growth marked by justice.[9] Taken together, and mindful of the question above, they may in fact recommend much needed perspective on one of the greatest challenges to Black Christian thought and practice.

"Somebodyness" and the Theological Significance of the Body

In spite of persistent evil that challenged what he assumed was God's intentions for God's people, King maintained a perception of ultimate good—of a teleological sense of history—put in place and guided by a personal God. While this position "preached" (and continues to "preach") well and served as a source of moral and ethical determination, in light of persistent moral evil it frames one of our strongest theological challenges: Moral evil housed within the continuing struggle for life as signification of liberation discourse. Yet, perhaps in part our dilemma stems from a misread of what is most theologically valuable about King's view on the religious underpinning and theological signs of progress.

A careful read of King's theological insights suggests the manner in which the (Black) human body itself provides compelling evidence of

---

9. I imagine there is little doubt such is the case with King. However, for work on how this is also true for African American Humanism see Pinn, *By These Hands*. Furthermore, it should be noted that I am not offering a full description of King's thought and its genesis. I am not a King scholar, but rather one who studies African American religious thought and religiosity from a variety of angles and through some attention to a variety of figures. A more "authoritative" take on King's intellectual formulation is the task of others working on a different type of project.

progress toward liberation.[10] But this requires a delicate theological balance: Too much attention to the value of the body can result in the type of humanism King feared and rejected. Too little attention to the value of the body as benchmark of God's activity can result in a groundless and romantic faith that forfeits any sense of the world's importance—an otherworldly orientation that does not push for felt change within our historical moment. Over against the latter, King's approach promotes aesthetic considerations as theological insight, thereby highlighting the vitality of embodiment. "Somebodyness" conceptually grounds this approach, and it bears both theological and existential significance in that it suggests an alternate placement of Black bodies in time and space—a rethinking of the dual nature of the body—as symbol and as biochemical reality. The body takes on a new meaning, a new value and new importance that trump troubled historical relations. God provides resources for the revitalization of the *imago dei*—the reviving of the human—as new perception of the body's meaning and historical placement.

The demand for sociopolitical and economic restructuring is only the residue of this revamping of human *being* in that it is first measured by an increased sense of complex subjectivity couched in acknowledgement of the Black body's radiant beauty. In the words of a popular religious song, "I looked at my hands and they looked new. I looked at my feet and they did too"; and in King's words:

> This sense of *somebodyness* means the refusal to be ashamed of being black. Our children must be taught to stand tall with their heads proudly lifted. We need not be duped into purchasing bleaching creams that promise to make us lighter. We need not process our hair to make it appear straight. Whether some men, black and white, realize it or not, black people are very beautiful . . . The Negro, through self-acceptance and self-appreciation, will one day cause white America to see that integration is not an obstacle, but an opportunity to participate in the beauty of diversity.[11]

"Somebodyness" as theological concept promotes dynamic embodiment as the proper response to moral evil. That is to say, opposition to moral evil understood as the warping of humanity involves a reconstituting of the human. "With this new sense of 'somebodyness' and self-respect,"

---

10. This is a topic I take up in some detail in "King and the Civil Rights Movement," forthcoming.

11. King, *Where Do We Go from Here?* 123.

King recounts, "a new Negro has emerged with a new determination to achieve freedom and humanity dignity whatever the cost may be. This is the true meaning of the struggle that is taking place in the south today."[12] Again, aesthetic transformation vis-à-vis "somebodyness" and a new ontology are followed in time by felt and functional shifts in sociopolitical and economic reality. And the ultimate triumph of God's will in human history is known through the placement of these reconstituted bodies in the "Beloved Community."

King and the Personal God

Tied to this theological anthropology is the doctrine of God developed within academic reflection and Black Church-based praxis. In the final analysis King held to a radical sense of optimism in the face of profound suffering, but wrestled with the proper correlation between God's power and purpose in human history.[13] In a real way he came to rest theologically on a notion of God's power as "sufficient power to accomplish the most noble ends or purposes in cooperation with created persons."[14] Couched in this stance is a shift away from strict omnipotence to an understanding of God as having "matchless power."[15] In other words and in light of continuing existential realities, God's power is best understood as entailing ability beyond that of humans; but it is not a traditional sense of God's power as limitless. The goodness, love, righteousness and so on that characterize God for most African American Christian theists remain intact for King. Yet, the manner in which they are expressed in human history is reconsidered. What is more, King's sense of God and God's presence in the world necessitates attention to the body as both gauge of change and tool of transformation. In a word, King's God, as civil rights activism makes clear, requires human participation in order to bring about the "good."

As a Humanist, I appreciate this taming of the God concept in ways that foster accountability and responsibility on the part of humans—through an appeal to the dignity of personality. This reformulation does not provide necessarily a sustainable shift away from the dilemma of

---

12. King, "The Case against 'Tokenism,'" 108.

13. I am indebted to Rufus Burrows's work on King's "Personalism." Burrows, *God and Human Dignity*, 99–100.

14. Ibid., 101.

15. Ibid., 106, 111–13.

redemptive suffering that marks much Black Christian thought. King preaches and promotes the importance of the human person, but not in a way that allows for tenaciously safeguarding said body against unmerited suffering. To the contrary, pain endured is often noted as a mechanism for refining the human. In this regard, King's theology might be said to simply affirm a long tradition of redemptive suffering argumentation that litters the religious/theological geography of African American communities. This, however, is not the only option when reading King. And it is this other option that might push the Black Church into a more productive posture over against William Jones's insightful critique.

What if one gives center stage to a sometimes minority perspective within King's thought? What if one were to highlight the theological posture with which King flirted as a student, that of his Boston University professor Edgar Brightman?[16] According to Brighman, God can "actualize the good," this remains the domain of the divine, but this ability does not preclude shifts in plan and strategy on the part of God. The purpose in breaking into human history, as liberation theologians want to put it, remains clearly focused on the good.[17] This theological posture, however, prioritizes God's overall agenda, not every divine actions and maneuver found within that large framework. And in this way, God's power does not prevent missteps, wrong turns (albeit even these point to God's deep desire to help humanity). Penultimate events related to God's agenda are not guaranteed effective. Humans also fall short at times, willing evil rather than good.[18] In this sense, for instance, King might explain the failed Albany (Georgia) campaign as one such move, a strategy that did not point to ultimate failure of "right" over "evil," but rather a moment during which the partnership between humans and God did not bear fruit.

This is not a simple restating of William R. Jones's brilliant critique of Black theology's theodical pronouncements.[19] Rather, what I offer suggests a restructuring of God's power in ways that allows for maintenance

---

16. Burrows's work on this topic is referenced throughout this chapter. Readers should also give attention, for example, to Lewis Baldwin's *There Is a Balm in Gilead: The Cultural Roots of Martin Luther King, Jr.* Also see Carson, "Martin Luther King, Jr., and the African-American Social Gospel," 159–77; Hill, *The Theology of Martin Luther King, Jr. and Desmond Mpilo Tutu*; Dorrien, *The Making of American Liberal Theology.*

17. Burrows, *God and Human Dignity*, 96–121.

18. Ibid., 99–100.

19. Jones, *Is God a White Racist?*

of the God concept but also recognizes shortcomings in divine interaction with humans. For Jones this begs the question of racism; but in the context of this chapter it points to missteps and not a fundamental questioning of the divine. *This is because these missteps are followed by new strategies and maneuvers.* A racist deity, one could argue, would exercise power in a more consistently demonic manner and this would be present in the development of human history.[20] Furthermore, as I have noted elsewhere, the Humanist measures the shape and potential of what can be known, thereby giving the small and large—both mundane—activities of life significance that shapes them into movements of ritual importance. On the other hand, the Black Church is concerned with the promise of the past reflected in Christ and future hope represented in human redemption; and, the present moment is measured against the past and the future so conceived.[21] The Black Church's framing of salvation history requires this formulation. However, this formulation can be modified without great harm to its theological integrity and inner logic.

A shift in doctrine of God, combined with mild Humanist sensibilities, may offer a way to maintain theistic commitments without a glorification of human suffering as redemptive. One can continue to claim God is loving, kind, just, and committed to the welfare of those who suffer. Here is the difference: Black theologians have assumed, however, that this assortment of characteristics necessitates an understanding that all events enacted by such a God must lead directly to the desired end. Even King notes that God is the best example of personality, of action, and faithfulness.[22] Nonetheless, for King this involves the best of these traits, not the perfection of these traits. In a word, God—even as "matchless" in character and capability—may shift perspective, change direction, "repent"

---

20. A distinction between this Humanist perspective and that of Black liberation theology involves the nature of passion and urgency involved with both—the deeply disturbed tone of Black liberation theologies and the more measured, dispassionate tone of Humanist theological formulations. This difference does not stem from a lack of concern with oppression and the oppressed within Humanist theological frameworks. Rather, it stems from Humanists' recognition of the absurd nature of life, and the notion that we construct this world alone, without divine guidance and the balance—the hopefulness of hope—such guidance provides.

21. I link this notion to William Jones in "William R. Jones and Religiously Justified Conduct," forthcoming, as well as to notions of a Humanist response to Christian salvation: "A Beautiful *Be-ing*," 19–36.

22. Burrows, "Personalism," 221.

for decisions made without losing status as the best knower and doer—the ultimate source of our understanding of freedom and the framework for our sense of relationship and community (as "Beloved Community").

In light of King's framing of the issue, I cannot resist raising a question: What might be the look of Black and Womanist theologies if they were to take seriously the type of God concept opened through King's theology, and were to use it to interrogate continuing modalities of discrimination?

Reenvisioning the Divine

Black and Womanist theologies maintain recognition of moral evil as real and felt—as a problem. And they are clear on the role of humans in perpetuating this problem. The challenge, however, has involved the best way to theologically place God in relationship to this moral evil. It is in regard to this sticking point that the Christ Event is viewed by most Black and Womanist theologians as being of deep and lasting significance.[23] To be sure, in some significant ways Black and Womanist theologies are an extended Christology in that everything flows through this category because, according to James Evans, "in essence, Jesus mediates the ungivenness of God, bringing God into the sphere of our existence. Jesus liberates us form the crushing burden of otherness and difference, bringing to light the God in us. In so doing, Jesus makes possible a way of life—a mode of praxis—grounded in faith, assurance, and obedience."[24] Or, as Cone notes, Christianity "begins and ends" with Jesus, all theological reflection on this faith must stem from and reach back to the Christ Event.[25]

For the sake of argument I return to a theological shift by Kelly Brown Douglas mentioned in the first chapter, one going further than most Black and Womanist thought but not as far as Delores Williams's analysis of atonement in which she argues there is no cosmic glory in blood and no benefit in death. Douglas, by means of this theological shift, argues for a

---

23. Examples of this perspective include Grant, *White Women's Christ and Black Women's Jesus*; Terrell, *Power in the Blood?*; Douglas, *The Black Christ*; and Goatley, *Were You There?*

24. Evans, *We Have Been Believers*, 97–98.

25. This argument is found in Cone's first two books, but for the purposes of this essay, I reference this discussion of Christology in light of his response to William R. Jones. See Cone, *God of the Oppressed*, fn. 23, 267–68.

middle way—an appreciation for the implications of suffering that run just shy of an endorsement of redemptive suffering.[26] Such a stance is possible in that, according to Douglas, God was opposed to the crucifixion of Christ. However, and this is vital, opposition did not result in God's stopping the event, nor did it result in an alteration (or modification) of the pain involved. One might ask if this was because God—consistent with a larger logic—did not prevent or stop the crucifixion in order to allow for a greater good; or, was it because God could not stop the crucifixion? Avoiding this question, Douglas instead seeks to theologically redefine and reconceive God's relationship to suffering. She suggests God's answer to suffering is found not in the pain of Christ but in the triumph of the resurrection.

The connections to Williams's critique of atonement are clear. Like Williams, Douglas downplays the redemptive nature of the actual crucifixion and highlights the ways in which this event points beyond itself (for Williams it points backward, and for Douglas it points forward). According to Williams, the importance of the Christ Event is firmly lodged in the ministry of Christ. It is the ethical and liberative outreach of Christ that Christians are to model, not the suffering. For Douglas the importance of the Christ Event is found ultimately in openness to new possibilities of relationship brought about by Christ's triumph over death. Through this resurrection, humanity meets God anew.

Williams works to jettison the cross because it is a sign of human misconduct, the death-dealing activities of humanity. However, Douglas's take on the Christ Event still goes through the cross. As a result, Douglas's formulation makes unavoidable a question: "is there any positive, empowering value for a suffering people to be found in a religion with an unjust execution at its center?" Her response: "I contend that there is."[27]

A point of clarification is necessary so as to avoid the assumption that Douglas invites imitation of Christ's pain. Douglas does not render the act of suffering privileged experience. She instead gives suffering meaning by rendering important the body of those who suffer. The death and resurrection of Christ speaks new meaning to embodied African Americans in that God enters the world through a despised body and redeems the world through the maintained integrity of that body. Nonetheless, this centering of the Christ Event frames liberation discourse for Douglas, but

26. Williams, *Sisters in the Wilderness.*

27. Douglas, *What's Faith Got to Do with It?* 96.

also troubles this discourse in that the cross follows close on the heels of a revolutionary ministry. Perhaps the resurrection makes too fine a point between the activity of the cross and the shape of ministry. Is this stance sufficient?

In light of the Christ Event, to continue to speak of God and all this commitment implies must entail for theologically-minded Black liberationists recognition of both death and life. The latter is present in vibrant ways in their theology, and death too—but only as the precursor to a continuing transcendence—the removal of God in order for God to reappear. This, however, has done little to address fundamental issues related to moral evil and theodicy. And while Williams and Douglas wrestle with this dilemma, more typical responses—beyond silence—often entail talk of God in louder terms, as if volume and passion can substitute for substance and historically situated presence.

Certainly Black and Womanist theologians are not alone in this struggle to speak of God, and in fact they have some rather unlikely companionship. For instance, "Death of God" theologians like Thomas J. J. Altizer, it seems, tried to address such dilemmas by claims that God is "dead." By this attention-grabbing statement he meant: in the Christ Event God completely empties God's self into the world, and the spirit of God is not resurrected but defused through the world.[28] Black and Womanist theologians will want to follow him only so far on this path in that what Altizer pushed for does not recognize the demonic nature of oppression, oppression that blocks this unity between God and world.[29] What might offend Black and Womanist theologians in particular, and Black Christians in general, is not the process of God's emptying into the world, but rather it is the language used to describe this event. God is infused in human history through Christ, and humans participate in this divinity to the extent they take on—in an ontological sense—God's character. The divine is submerged in the context of human suffering and in so becoming removes the transcendent element: God emptied God's self, and imploded transcendence for the sake of humanity.

---

28. See, for example, Altizer and Hamilton, *Radical Theology and the Death of God*.

29. Howard Thurman probably comes closest within African American thought to this ideal relationship between God and world, but even he recognizes the manner in which racism, for instance, blocks our ability to achieve such the blurring of boundaries of self in all. See Thurman, *Deep Is the Hunger*; Thurman, *With Head and Heart*; Thurman, *Jesus and the Disinherited*; and Thurman, *The Inward Journey*.

While many liberation theologians of color would find problematic Altizer's charged pronouncement (referred to as the "Death of God"), I believe they would agree with the notion that God allows God's self to be absorbed into the world for humanity's sake. The proposition that God kills God's self in the Christ Event is a work of theodicy meant to explain an apparent silence in the face of moral evil. In short, in killing God's self, God has done the work for us, saving us from the task. But does this offer us anything substantive in terms of our moral-evil dilemma? Based on continued oppression faced by African Americans, did God's plan for improvement fail?

God's self-sacrifice did not stem the tide of destruction. God remains good and just—traits of central importance to liberation theologians—but has taken a tack that in fact has done little to change the plight of African Americans who continue to suffer. Was the Christ Event the final word, or even a proper word?

Divine Mishaps and Detours

Perhaps the notion of "divine mishaps and detours" is the best available way of addressing the dilemmas and questions raised above. Yet what might be most objectionable about this theological stance is the manner in which it entertains, no, requires, an acceptance of a God whose plan develops in awkward and bulky stages, in fits and starts.

This God takes sides and is concerned with liberation. It is not the motivation or commitment of this God that is questioned; rather, it is recognition of this God's activities as incomplete. God's work is unfinished, perhaps flawed in part because this God's liberative work is experimental—changing and often reactive, demonstrating commitment and concern but guaranteeing little. God interacts with humans in ways involving self-correction, changed plans and paths. According to this scheme, God is deeply attached to and committed to the welfare of humanity—but perhaps at times through penultimate events that fail to provide a positive resolution.

In terms of application, this stance involves an alternate perspective on Christology through acknowledgment of the Christ Event as penultimate, as a marker of God's posture toward the world as opposed to a conclusive response to modern modalities of oppression. The Christ Event has limited constructive reach. The Event was incomplete, inconclusive, serving as a marker of God's ability and commitment unfulfilled in our historical moment. And an embrace of it by Black Christians might be seen as entailing an act of faith, but not as traditionally perceived. Faith here involves moving through the world as if God has already acted again—living in anticipation of continued activity on the part of God, activity that will be significant.

There is another dimension to this posture in that faith here involves *dynamic forgiveness*: Black theists forgiving God for God's miscalculation.

This is difficult: How is forgiveness the proper way to frame human posture toward God? Moral evil is not simply free will out of control; current circumstances also arise from miscalculation on God's part. It is not to say that God cannot be held accountable because God is not omnipotent. Rather, *God is held accountable, not because God did not act, but because God's actions simply shifted the problem*. God's approach has not worked, if liberation (as Black and Womanist theologies suggest) is the norm. *Hence, God's good intentions must be recognized and the shortcomings of God's activity noted without resentment*.

In so doing, dynamic forgiveness is exercised: dynamic because it is infused with a strong sense of purpose and a matter of forgiveness in that it entails behavior interrogated and pardoned. In a certain way this is a pointing out of a hopeful emptiness, of absence but in ways that call for humans to fill the void as best they can. The doctrine of God becomes anthropology writ large.

This is what the Christ Event might mean when King's theology and my Humanist sensibilities are brought together. There is, however, a necessary step in addition to dynamic forgiveness: God's contrition is needed and might be represented by a move on God's part, another strong act in partnership with humanity that signals—as did the Christ Event—the concern of God for justice and liberation.

So Then . . .

The tenacious nature of moral evil, as encountered during King's ministry and as still present in all too many pockets of misery, requires creative and focused theological attention. As King demonstrated, such thinking must involve a flexible intellectual posture, one that is open to new possibilities made available through any number of theological positions. It is this prioritizing of felt need over reified theological frameworks that fostered in King a deep appreciation for and profound wrestling with various modalities of Personalism.

While this perspective on Personalism is helpful, it is my belief that the impact of such a theological position within African American circles is further enhanced through attention to the humanizing dimension offered by Humanist sensibilities. In this way every element of our theological framework is interrogated and held accountable for its role in the fostering of healthy life options. But what is more, a combining of King's Personalism and African American Humanism allows for a deep appreciation of the troubled nature of our life journey—a sensitivity to the manner in which our fight against moral evil is complex and the cartography of our struggles full of meandering theological routes and religious pitfalls, as well as markers of promise and hope.

6

Hitting Where It Hurts

Rethinking Protest against Gender Bias in Black Churches

THE BLACK CHURCH TRADITION is marked by a troubling and embarrassing problem, one that has been in place for centuries—gender-based discrimination. The story is well known, having been chronicled in numerous books and articles. Furthermore, it is clearly present in the doctrines, sermons, and actions of ministers and congregations from as early as the formal development of independent Black churches. Fueled by the residue of the cult of domesticity, the need for male-centered leadership as the proper framing for spiritual development in line with the will of God (and perhaps as a corrective to the social stigma of race) was voiced without apology. The avenues of involvement in Black churches available to women were restricted and restricting, and reflected a damaging synergy between race and gender.[1]

In this final chapter, I offer a method for resolving the problem of gender-based discrimination. What I propose may not alter fully the attitudes of some within Black Church circles. Problematic perspectives on the level of individual members will persist. But what I suggest here will promote non-gender-based criteria for church leadership, and as a consequence it will increase opportunities for the full involvement of women in once restricted areas of Black churches.

Setting the Scene

It is at times the case that sexism as a marker of gender-based discrimination within Black churches is perceived to be premised upon a turning

---

1. Gilkes, "The Politics of 'Silence,'" 84–86.

away from a more egalitarian perspective on religious work, and resulting from African Americans embracing the sexist organization that marked the churches and social structures of the dominant society.[2] This take on the problem is misguided in that, although we cannot fully know the workings of the "invisible institution," we know even during the period of slavery gender-based discriminatory practices were in place. From the early stages of the Black Church's development to the present, there have been dimensions of church work available to women, and this could include opportunities to speak within the context of the congregation.[3] But this access was restricted and did not circumvent a more important prohibition—a denial of formal ministerial orders *qua* ordination. In this way, Richard Allen, the first leader of the African Methodist Episcopal Church, and others like him placed the preaching abilities of women within the context of a larger logic concerning the "look" of an ordained minister. This look was socially inscribed and biblically based. The "look" was both materially and metaphorically rendered as the Black male, and deviation from this could only be allowed as a matter of short-term exceptions.[4] Resulting from this situation was what Cheryl Townsend Gilkes refers to as the "politics of silence," or the safeguarding of key roles and functions within the church setting for men.[5]

This particular depiction of authenticity with respect to ministry was not met with silence. African American women from the very for-

---

2. Gilkes, *"If It Wasn't for the Women . . . ,"* 200.

3. It must be noted that Black Spiritual churches developed during the early twentieth century present a counter example in that they were often initiated and run by women. For example, Mother Leafy Anderson is credited for much of this movement's development in Louisiana. See, for example: Jacobs and Kaslow, *The Spiritual Churches of New Orleans*. A similar situation—women in key leadership positions—is also evidenced in some of the smaller Pentecostal and nondenominational churches, as well as in the New Thought Movement. A key example with respect to the latter would be Rev. Dr. Johnnie Coleman of Christ Unity Temple. See Martin, *Beyond Christianity*; Martin, "New Thought," 2009.

4. While relevant works are presented throughout this chapter, those interested in a description of the gender problem should see, for example, Cone and Wilmore, *Black Theology: A Documentary History* 1:279–348 (part 5); Cone and Wilmore, *Black Theology: A Documentary History* 2:257–354 (part 4); Gilkes, *"If It Wasn't for the Women . . ."*; Williams, *Sisters in the Wilderness*; Cone, *For My People*; Higginbotham, *Righteous Discontent*; Douglas, *Sexuality and the Black Church*; Hayes, *Hagar's Daughters*; Lincoln and Mamiya, *The Black Church in the African American Experience*.

5. Gilkes, "The Politics of 'Silence,'" 81.

mation of ministerial roles during the antebellum period to the present moment have critiqued this discriminatory framework. The following words spoken by Jarena Lee, a woman seeking ministerial opportunities, are familiar; their passion and insight haunting, and their demands clear: "O how careful ought we to be, lest through our by-laws of church government and discipline, we bring into disrepute even the word of life. For as unseemly as it may appear nowadays for a woman to preach, it should be remembered that nothing is impossible with God. And why should it be thought impossible, heterodox, or improper, for a woman to preach? Seeing the Saviour died for the women as well as the man. If a man may preach, because the Saviour died for him, why not the woman? Seeing he died for her also."[6] Florence Spearing Randolph shares a similar sentiment over one hundred years later: "But notwithstanding the fact that the first gospel message delivered to the women," she says, "there always has been and still is great antipathy to women preachers. But God, with whom there is neither Jew nor Greek, bond nor free, male nor female, in His wonderful plan of salvation has called and chosen men and women according to His divine will as laborers together with Him for the salvation of the world."[7]

These laments, the first offered to Black Methodists in the early nineteenth century and the latter given in 1930 by a member of the African Methodist Episcopal Zion Church, set a tone both in shaping the problem of gender-based discrimination and in suggesting a strategy for countering this form of oppression.

Biblical Authority as Justification: Wor(l)d Formation

Even a superficial reading of Lee and Randolph, as but two of many possible examples, suggests both the restriction on and the rationale for women in ordained ministry rest on biblical and theological grounds. For example, while the politics of family structure and notions of domesticity are often mentioned, these are but tangential arguments in that they are held to be correct based on biblical and theological authority. Furthermore, to the degree normative social arrangements—the gender status quo—are referenced, they function as authoritative only to the extent they are perceived as being in line with biblical and theological precedence.

---

6. Lee, "My All to Preach the Gospel," 7.

7. Randolph, "Antipathy to Women Preachers," 127.

This appeal to the Bible should come as no surprise based on the centrality of scriptural paradigms and "biblical warrant," as some have phrased it, for the formation of the fundamental dynamics of Black Church culture. There is in operation here an assumption that problems within Black churches are not endemic, and its spiritual ethos means changes must be approached biblically and theologically because the church is not first and foremost governed by a secular agenda. "The Bible says" is a statement lending authority to any argument, and it is authority articulated theologically but with wide-ranging ramifications for a full range of church structures, behaviors, and practices.

As scholars Theophus Smith and Allen Callahan have noted with great insight, the Bible has served as an organizing principle, a means by which the moral and ethical insights of African Americans have been presented. For Smith, it provided the necessary material of conjuration in that it could be deciphered and used by the wise to radically change their predicament. "Here the sacred text of Western culture, the Bible," Smith writes, "comes to view as a magical formulary for African Americans; a book of ritual prescriptions for reenvisioning and, therein transforming history and culture."[8] *In this regard, biblical interpretation becomes a wor(l)d shaping activity in that it both provides the language for naming our values and gives substance and meaning to our spaces of encounter.* Within the context of Black Church tradition, this notion of biblical interpretation gives contextual importance to mantras such as "the Bible teaches . . ."

Callahan begins *The Talking Book* by noting the deep and immediate connection between African Americans and the Bible. Posing the intersection in sharp terms, "African Americans," Callahan notes, "are the children of slavery in America. The Bible, as no other book, is the book of slavery's children."[9] For Black Christians, this Bible served as a blueprint for protest as noted in the slave rebellions of figures like Gabriel Prosser and Nat Turner, and provided a typology for the reconstruction of identity over against the dehumanization of enslavement. In these and other ways, the Bible provided an opportunity for deconstruction of oppressive realities and situations; but it also provided the rationale and mechanisms for construction—the forging of alternate structures of meaning and patterns of relationship.

---

8. Smith, *Conjuring Culture*, 3.

9. Callahan, *The Talking Book*, xi.

Pervasive throughout African American culture, as Callahan suggests, the Bible has played a special role in the formation and function of Black Christian culture—particularly the thinking and workings of Black churches. The ethical and moral outlook of these churches and the manner in which they frame and "fix" (as in both to situate firmly and to resolve) questions of place and conduct draw from this sacred text.

As a religious obstruction against women in formal positions of church ministry and leadership, the Bible was said to provide explicit regulations and passages of Scripture were picked out for this purpose. Take, for example, 1 Corinthians 14:34–35: "Let the women keep silence in the churches: for it is not permitted unto them to speak; but let them be in subjection, as also saith the law. And if they would learn anything, let them ask their own husbands at home: for it is shameful for a woman to speak in the church." Or, 1 Timothy 2:11–15, where the following is found: "Let a woman learn in quietness with all subjection. But I permit not a woman to teach, nor to have dominion over a man, but to be in quietness. For Adam was first formed, then Eve; and Adam was not beguiled, but the woman being beguiled hath fallen into transgression: but she shall be saved through the childbearing, if they continue in faith and love and sanctification with sobriety." In both cases, the implication is a sanctioned and fixed restriction on women within the Christian faith community that limits female involvement in church to supporting roles.[10]

Furthermore, one sees reliance on these "biblical warrants" in creedal commitments to male-led ministry. The Church of God in Christ, for instance, has this perspective on the centrality of Scripture: "We believe that the Bible is the Word of God and contains one harmonious and sufficiently complete system of doctrine. We believe in the full inspiration of the Word of God. We hold the Word of God to be the only authority in all matters and assert that no doctrine can be true or essential, if it does not find a place in this Word."[11] And while the Church of God in Christ—the largest African American Pentecostal denomination in the United States—contains numerous examples of women involved in the preaching ministry, these women tend to be exceptions to the general rule. For instance, according to the church's manual:

---

10. The problem of gender-based discrimination is not limited to Black churches. However, my concern in this volume is with the impact of such discrimination on women within Black churches.

11. "The Doctrine of the Church of God in Christ."

> The Church of God in Christ recognizes the scriptural impor-
> tance of women in the Christian ministry (Matthew 28:1; Mark
> 16:1; Luke 24:1; John 20:1); the first at the tomb on the morn-
> ing of Christ's resurrection; the first to whom the Lord appeared
> (Matthew 28:9; Mark 16:9; John 20:14); the first to announce the
> fact of the resurrection to the chosen disciples (Luke 29:9; 10:22)
> etc. But nowhere can we find a mandate to ordain women to
> be an Elder, Bishop, or Pastor. Women may teach the gospel to
> others (Philippians 4:3; Titus 2:3–5; Joel 2:28), have charge of a
> church in the absence of its Pastor, if the Pastor so wishes (Roman
> 16:1–5) without adopting the title of Elder, Reverend, Bishop or
> Pastor. Paul styled the women who labored with him as servants or
> Helpers, not Elders, Bishops, or Pastors. Therefore the Church of
> God In Christ cannot accept the following scriptures as a mandate
> to ordain women preachers: Joel 2:28; Galatians 3:28–29; Matthew
> 28:9–11.[12]

Because the Baptist tradition safeguards the authority of the local congregation, one is less likely to find the formal and wide-reaching statements
concerning women in ministry noted regarding the Church of God in
Christ. However, this does not mean there is not something resembling
systematic exclusion. Furthermore, as of the twentieth century, the three
major Methodist denominations each had official policy that made ordained ministry available to women. However, it is still often the case
that women who achieve ordination are hard pressed to secure church
appointments as senior pastor, if they do these pastorates are typically of
struggling churches. In these two cases, biblical warrant does not prevent
total participation, but rather serves to limit the quality and quantity of
opportunities.

In all cases, roles occupied by women and men within Black churches are discussed using a grammar and vocabulary couched in theological categories such as ecclesiology and theological anthropology, with
the Bible informing the content and form of these categories. Therefore,
ecclesiology asserts that the proper church, the true church, is guided by
these roles and is marked by the biblically sanctioned activities of men
and women within their respective roles. Meanwhile, theological anthropology informs this situation through an understanding of original sin by
which the fall of humanity is placed squarely on the shoulders of women.

---

12. *Official Manual with the Doctrines and Discipline of the Church of God in Christ*,
159–60.

As the biblical account is interpreted through this lens, the failure of Eve to abide by the will of God is punished. This follows on the heels of the creation of women as a help met to man, but as one under the authority of man. Such an understanding of women, when grounded in the biblical text and expressed theologically, is given a reified status as a marker of proper religious orientation and alignment with the will of God regarding the formation and nurture of community (including religious community).

Patriarchal readings of Scripture were given primary authority in that it was argued women were responsible for the fundamental shortcomings of humanity and men, then, were placed in the position of correcting for this initial harm done by women. The patriarchal arrangements in the Bible were read unto African Americans and played out in Black churches.[13] In response to this reading of Scripture, failure to play out one's role as drawn from the biblical text often meant feelings of failure, a questioning of one's religious identity and the strength of one's spiritual commitments.[14] It is understood that the work of women in churches is vital, the stuff of the organization's survival; but this does not entail in most cases recognition of this work involving the highest spiritual authority. It is interesting to note that seldom has attention been given to arguments revolving around abilities of women to perform particular tasks (such as preaching). Rather, talent might be acknowledged but it was outdone by biblical arguments and shadowed by theological rhetoric.[15]

When sexist views concerning women in ministry are voiced within African American Baptist and Methodist churches the grounding for such positions, as in Church of God in Christ, is premised on biblical pronouncements believed to not only justify but also require male dominance

---

13. One of the most effective means by which to reenforce this perspective was and remains the sermon. A charismatic message delivered on a Sunday could support activism regarding issues of race, but at the same time represent a church posture toward gender discrimination represented by attempts to "block efforts of women to move beyond traditional church roles, or to reject women clergy for doctrinal or theological reasons . . . Thus, church ideology may acknowledge the importance of equality in the secular arena, but give precedence to the complementary nature of women and men (rather than equality) in the spiritual arena" (Barnes, "Whosoever Will Let Her Come," 373). For information on how this might work, see Barnes, "Black Church Culture and Community Action," 967–94.

14. Ellison, "Are Religious People Nice People?" 411–30.

15. Gilkes, "The Politics of 'Silence,'" 98.

of the preached ministry. As voiced by both women and men within these churches, biblical living requires strict adherence to gender roles; and, this is all expressed through a theology of labor divisions, which maintains a general suspicion toward women as both physically and spiritually dangerous.

Countering Biblical Authority: Reversing the Wor(l)d

From the early Black Church during the period of slavery to the present, some men and women fought against this gender restrictive sense of legitimate (pastoral) leadership. And they worked to counter gender-based discrimination through an alternate read of Scripture and an alternate theological discourse. This process of using Scripture to combat exclusion is evidenced in the early writings of African American women. Take for example the words of Maria Stewart, who in the early 1800s became the first African American woman to lecture publicly on political issues. Marilyn Richards argues that "the women Stewart approvingly spoke of early in her career, wives and mothers who exercised influence upon their husbands and through them perhaps in some way upon the world beyond the home, are replaced in her later work by examples of biblical and historical figures who wield genuine power and authority . . ."[16]

Stewart works through Scripture and reads it in light of a hermeneutic of African American women's need. In this way she is able to counter the typical read of St. Paul as restricting the public function of women. "Did St. Paul," she says, "but know of our wrongs and deprivations, I presume he would make no objections to our pleading in the public for our rights. Again, holy women ministered unto Christ and the apostles; and women of refinement in all ages, more or less, have had a voice in moral, religious and political subjects."[17] Continuing this appeal to Scripture, Evelyn Brooks Higginbotham insightfully remarks women during the late nineteenth and early twentieth century fought their exclusion through what she labels a "feminist theology." Higginbotham is not suggesting these women created full and systematic theological programs. Rather, African American churchwomen during the late nineteenth and early twentieth centuries developed a somewhat structured and consistent theological

---

16. Stewart, *Maria C. Stewart*, 25.

17. Ibid., 68.

argument that made use of their experience and the gospel demand for equality. They promoted a woman-centered interpretation of what God requires of God's church. In short, they made use of Scripture and theological language to promote the feminization of work for God.[18]

Arguing from either an implicit or explicit contextualization of Scripture, proponents of women in ordained ministry argued the biblical text must be read in light of its particular cultural world, in light of its particular historical context. This interpretative practice pushes against efforts to read the Bible literally and instead asserts the authority of the Bible only in relationship to the needs of the people. This view exposes the patriarchal tone of the Bible and restricts its impact by pointing beyond proof texts supporting male authority. So arranged it promotes a general ethos of equality within the spiritual worlds of the Bible. There is, to quote the Bible, "no male or female" and God is "no respecter of persons" in the work of spreading the good news of salvation through Christ.

This is a position guided by a theological rhetoric of willing service. The Church of God is understood as benefiting from the labor of all, based on talents observed and not gender. The theological assumption that women are inherently flawed and rightfully restricted to certain supporting roles in the church is interrogated, challenged, and superceded by a litmus test of proven results: Mary Magdalene was the first to witness to the risen Lord, thereby setting in motion a long line of women preachers of God's gift through Christ.

The Trouble with Double-Talk

Based on the above, I offer a word of caution: Theologically and biblically based arguments are useful if one is seeking spiritual consensus related to elements of a shared faith, things that one might examine while bracketing existential arrangements. However, the call for an end to gender-based discrimination is lodged *within* existential or mundane considerations and cannot be corrected through interpretation of Scripture and theological debate alone. This is because such argumentation does not call into question inherent discriminatory patterns in that theological argumentation is plastic in nature and can be fixed to any particular position. To the extent theology is understood rightly as a second order enterprise, it can be used

---

18. Higginbotham, *Righteous Discontent*, 1993; Cobble, *The Sex of Class*, 2–4.

to unpack or explain any given position taken. And, the biblical text can be positioned in support of any argument. Use of the Bible and theological rhetoric frames the discussion from the dominant group's perspective and merely seeks to rework their argument. When appealing to Scripture and theological counterarguments the goal must be constructed within the context of existing assumptions—greater representation. *I suggest the goal should be a total restructuring of power dynamics and the development of a logic of ministry that is more progressive and inclusive of difference and creative opportunity.*

Appeal to the Bible and its accompanying theological platform does not produce clear winners on this issue of sexism as mode of gender-based discrimination in the Black Church. How could it when the Bible is an open text? The ability to apply Scripture with attention to contextual concerns and by highlighting areas of agreement between the position being argued and the biblical text results in limited advancement of an argument on either side. Biblically formulated and theologically expressed debate on the subject of women's role in Black churches has produced no consensus for either position.

Outcomes: Limited Gains

It bears repeating that this arrangement has not meant a total impasse regarding women in the pulpit. Some denominations have women serving as pastor, and even Baptist Conventions and certain Pentecostal denominations have women pastoring churches. What is more common however, involves alternate modalities of participation and importance. As scholars such as Cheryl Townsend Gilkes have demonstrated with great skill, the dominance of males with respect to leadership roles does not mean Black women are without authority and "soft" forms of power within churches. Positions such as "church mother" suggest the ability to influence and persuade male leadership to think in certain ways and support certain positions that are of interest to at least some of the women in the church.[19] In addition, there are areas of church advancement such as missions that have historically relied on the expertise and energy of women for both labor and financial support. And as Josephine Carson noted in mid-twentieth-century South Carolina, "the women really don't

---

19. Gilkes, "The Politics of 'Silence,'" 105; Melvin D. Williams, *Community in a Black Pentecostal Church*, 60–61.

have much to say. They do a lot of the work, they cook for the picnic and socials, and they raise the most money and they kind of keep the church going, but then you get to policy, the men have it all tied up."[20]

Women manipulated opportunities with great creativity, preaching as missionaries, exhorters, teachers, and so on but without fundamental change to the rationale for their more formal exclusion from the pulpit. These roles, while showcasing talent, have not fostered wide-ranging and sustained alterations to the very conceptualization of church participation and authority. Furthermore, while these positions suggest somewhat porous boundaries within many churches, they do not provide enough to suggest such positions offer equivalent authority and power within Black Church settings. In a word, women occupying positions such as church mother and deaconess, or evangelist do not trouble the gender hierarchy and therefore do not call into question the gender politics of ministry in a substantial and damaging manner.

While some women have gained success in the preached ministry and positions of authority (such as the bishopric) within particular Black denominations, it is more commonly the case that women have limited access to ordained ministerial roles.[21] In addition, the establishment of special days such as "Women's Day" for women does little to challenge the general gender bias of church practice. Instead these special occasions circumscribe the proper outlets for women's talents. While acknowledging this limitation, Townsend Gilkes also finds within "woman-centered" activities the seeds of structural change. "At the same time," she writes, "the practice sidesteps the issue of permanent pastoral and denominational leadership within the institutions in which black women have invested so much time and money. Nevertheless, the final result is to ensure the presence of a woman-centered perspective in the life of the church; that perspective has occasionally even converted a pastor to the position of feminist advocacy."[22] F. E. Redwine makes a similar point when saying, "I very much fear the pastor would resign and the church doors would be closed, if there were no women in it. Woman's work, her prayers, her collection of influence in shaping the lives of children while they're young.

---

20. Quoted in Frederick C. Harris, *Something Within*, 164.

21. And some of those who have gained opportunities have done so by adopting to the best of their ability—through preaching style, religious politics, and other modes—those things considered markers of true (read patriarchal enforcing) leadership. By so doing, they seek to blur signs and symbols of gender difference.

22. Gilkes, "The Politics of 'Silence,'" 105.

Woman has been granted recognition in the Evangelistic work of the church and her profound interest as it was in Paul's time of preaching, has added much interest in the numerical and spiritual as well as financial strength of the Church."[23] Nonetheless, the dominant group's perspective maintains always at least passive adherence: The Black Church as a general phenomenon maintains gender-based discriminatory practices, justifies them biblically, and expresses them theologically.

Assessment: What Do You Really Want?

A sustainable and productive challenge to gender bias in Black churches requires clarity regarding the primary markers—benchmarks—of full inclusion. What do Black women and their male sympathizers want?[24] Response to this question tends to develop in terms of access to formal outlets to ordained ministry. There is good reason for this in that the late twentieth century marked a staggering increase in the number of women entering seminary with the hope of achieving a pastorate. In terms of percentage increases, Delores Carpenter suggests almost a 700 percent increase in the number of Black women securing seminary degrees for the twelve years between 1972 and 1984.[25] Clearly Black and White women saw in civil rights legislation opportunity to forge new positions in church ministry, with the first stop being seminaries. In some cases, women accounted for at least one-third of the total student body. Some denominations responded to changing social relations and political processes by (reluctantly) opening ordination to women, but ordination should not be understood as synonymous with full excess to the pulpit, particularly when in the African American mainline denominations only one percent of congregations are pastored by women.[26] The frustrations experienced

---

23. Collier-Thomas, *Daughters of Thunder*, 220.

24. According to a 1993 study, laity within the major Black denominations favor ordained ministry for women. Smaller numbers of clergy, particularly in Baptist and Pentecostal churches, support clerical opportunities for women. It is also interesting that some women within the laity of these denominations are opposed to women in ministry, and this is more often the case than with male laity. Even with this said, the percentage of women polled on this question and who answered in favor of ordained ministry is still relatively high. See Harris, *Something Within*, 164–68.

25. Referenced in Mamiya, *River of Struggle, River of Freedom*, 23.

26. Lehman, "Women's Path into Ministry," 7; Konieczny and Chaves, "Resources, Race, and Female-Headed Congregations in the United States," 261–71.

by these women and their efforts to address the disparate opportunities afford men and women became a major topic of conversation within Black Church circles, and served as a metasymbol of the Black Church's inadequacies. Participation in the ordained ministry remained restricted in part because criteria for involvement are understood theologically[27] and hence are easily countered by biblical warrants. Perhaps this accounts for the situation highlighted by Edward Lehman who writes, "especially after the radicalism of the early 1970s died down, only a minority of clergy women placed much importance on the idea of changing the sexism of the church."[28]

While the concern is not limited to the number of women in the pastorate, representation is vital and there are ways to mark the adequacy of representation. Regarding this point, the numerical dominance of women cannot be ignored and should urge a question: Do the positions and profiles of women within Black churches match the number of Black women in churches? Patterns of participation may vary based on the rural vs. urban context, and the southern vs. northern context, what seems to remain relatively consistent is the large percentage of Black women who compose the membership of local churches and denominations.[29] With respect to race, African Americans have asked for fair representation; why not this same demand in church work? Does the overall involvement of Black women[30] offer them a strong sense of their value and importance to these churches?

If the object for those protesting gender-based discrimination is development of more opportunities within the context of the existing gender-based arrangements as a means by which to secure a bigger slice of the ministerial "pie," then the current approach is effective vis-à-vis soft forms of authority and power combined with the occasional comprise of the boundary through a woman pastor, presiding elder or bishop.

However, if the desired outcome is fundamental and permanent change whereby gender is no longer the determining factor in professional inclusion and development, then a new strategy is necessary.

---

27. Lehman, "Women's Path into Ministry," 11.

28. Ibid.

29. Hunt and Hunt, "Regional Patterns of African American Church Attendance," 779–91; Hunt and Hunt, "Regional Religions?" 569–94.

30. Reese and Brown, "The Effects of Religious Messages on Racial Identity," 24–43; Chatters et al., "African American Religious Participation," 132–45.

The available literature (e.g., sermons and scholarly publications) suggest those seeking the ordination (and full ministerial rights) of women are interested in a complete reworking of church structure whereby gender is not a negative but simply a marker of difference allowing for various perspectives and creative possibilities. Regarding the latter, I argue we must begin with an examination of what we have meant by church "work." If the goal is to privilege "call" and effectiveness as criteria for church ministry involvement, and to do so in a way that does not denigrate existing modalities of involvement (e.g., deaconess, evangelist, missionary), then a new strategy is necessary, one that takes into consideration both the spiritual basis of the church and it's existence (and needs) as a business enterprise.

Rethinking Church "Work"

Again, I would suggest the mode of combat—biblically warrants and theological rhetoric—do not allow for deep damage to existing structures supporting discriminatory thinking and practice. This is not difficult to decipher and centuries of persistent gender-based discrimination, one might think, would have suggested the need for new and more aggressive strategies of engagement. Why has not this shift in process occurred in far reaching ways?

It is because of the way in which "work" is understood within the context of Black churches. Daphne Wiggins sums it up nicely when saying, "the church encourages female labor while according the highest positions of recognition to men. Stressing the virtues of humility and of rendering one's works to God without fanfare, the church holds at bay any personal dissatisfaction or stirrings of collective challenge."[31] Joan Martin, drawing on the antebellum context of Black women and using a Womanist lens, argues "work and labor are measured by self, familial, and community survival and nurture rather than by individual economic success or other values of the dominant society—values that oppress rather than liberate communities of black people."[32] In thinking through the nature of work, Martin provides a triadic structure. First, there is the work that God accomplishes with regard to "creation and redemption (liberation)" and this

---

31. Wiggins, *Righteous Content*, 185.

32. Joan M. Martin, *More Than Chains and Toil*, 77.

labor is outlined in Scripture. The second modality of work involves that which humans perform to meet life needs. And finally, there is the work of the church whereby the will of God is performed on earth consistent with the teachings of Christ.[33]

There are differing connections, but all forms of work have some bearing on religiosity. Hence, even mundane modalities of work have spiritual import. "Within the context of daily work," Martin remarks when reflecting on New Testament assumptions concerning work, "there is the opportunity to see one's work as a response to life rendered to God. Work for the Christian is a vocation—that is, a vehicle through which one is to be obedient to God, who is the Christian's master."[34] Furthermore, "Paul in particular is underlining the double use of the term vocation, or calling. Persons are 'called' into new life by God through repentance and faith and into the life and work of the church. This is the foundation from which Christians become 'workers' in whatever they do in daily, 'secular' activity."[35] Framed by a womanist read of the redemption of work by Protestant reformers, Martin argues because humans are in constant relationship to the world and to the divine, what humans do (e.g., work) is always connected to both humanity and God. Vocation and work are given spiritual importance and serve to express dimensions of God's demand on human life. This, however, is not to suggest all work has merit, or is "good" in that some labor is degrading and supportive of the status quo. On this point Martin's work dovetails with that of Delores Williams, whose brilliant analysis of forced and voluntary surrogacy serves to reenforce the troubled nature of work through which Black women are forced to serve the welfare of others during slavery and to continue serving the welfare of others after slavery because of economic hardship and limited work opportunities.[36] I say this while also acknowledging distinctions in their analysis in that Williams gives attention to both economic exploitation and sexual exploitation, while Martin's primary concern is sexist oppression within the context of employment.

Martin's perspective is meant to enliven the significance of Black women, and point out the manner in which work for them is defined by

---

33. Ibid., 113.

34. Ibid., 114.

35. Ibid.

36. Williams, *Sisters in the Wilderness*.

struggle against injustice and the push for personhood over against discrimination. Thinking about the experiences of enslaved women, Martin says, "in relation to exploitation, work was evil and caused suffering. In relation to resistance for self, family, and community in the midst of oppression, work was a source of faithful, moral living. Work was, in this way, about living and resisting the consequences of evil."[37] Furthermore, Martin states, "enslaved women believed that God willed work and labor in civil and political spheres as well as spiritual freedom."[38] Nonetheless, it is within the context of the church setting that the nature and meaning of work shifts away from a sense of labor for physical and psychological stability to a matter of building the Kingdom of God. It is rendered a form of sacred conduct.

Martin is critical of "secular" work that serves to entrench African Americans in oppressive situations. However, the condition of Black women in Black churches with respect to leadership opportunities is not seen as a problematic labor problem: "our participation with God in God's act of creative work must be carefully interpreted when we heed the impulse to make general theological-ethical statements. The work performed in enslavement (and in contemporary exploitative work) for the profits and power of unjust institutions cannot and should not be seen as inherently good work. Nor should it be seen as cocreative work with God."[39] Should not this critique apply to Black churches as well? It might, if work was not viewed within the context of the church as a spiritual concern and opportunity.

Work is spiritualized and rendered a service to God with benefits that are primarily connected to the building of the community of God.[40] In addition, like many volunteers, Black women tend to downplay if not deny the "cash value" of their church work because "they refuse to apply the utilitarian calculus to their volunteer contributions. The volunteer role is part of their identity. They believe they have no choice but to help."[41] Labor is not understood primarily as a matter of capitalist arrangement, an exchange of body energy for some type of material compensation.

37. Joan M. Martin, *More Than Chains and Toil*, 107.

38. Ibid., 108.

39. Ibid., 151.

40. Martin's interpretation of antebellum work frames labor as definable in theological terms because it is related to the *imago dei*—the divine/human relationship.

41. Musick et al., "Race and Formal Volunteering," 1542.

Rather, labor within the Black Church is typically viewed as the consequence of salvation and surrender to God through the community of the
like minded.[42]

Yet, on a very practical level, most churches are businesses and some
are even corporations with financial interests. But this is downplayed to
the extent Black Christians consider themselves "in the world, but not of
it." For the most part, monetary considerations become necessary materials for carrying out a more significant and theologically articulated mission to "save" the world. Offerings, tithes, special Sunday contributions,
fund raising, governmental money are understood as the raw material
by means of which the divinely inspired and mandated activities of the
church are financed.

The implications of this perspective are evident: there is in some
Black Christian circles an uneasy relationship with money based on how
some interpret this common mantra: "The love of money is the root of all
evil." Others offer Jesus chasing the moneychangers out the temple as evidence that one's relationship with money must be carefully monitored and
subordinated to soteriological considerations.[43] To the extent the business
dimension of churches is subordinate to their spiritual functions, and to
the degree church work or labor is spiritualized, theology remains the
language of protest and the Bible the primary battleground.

*If the church was strictly a spiritual enterprise without material at-
tachments to the world, labor and money might be of less importance. The
church, however, is a human enterprise with a mission that is in part cos-
mically oriented and situated; but it is also earthbound, a business enterprise with needs similar to other businesses.*[44] Therefore church work must
be understood as dualistic in nature and composed of two overlapping
realities. First, church work informs and makes possible the salvation-
based mission of churches. It allows the church to develop a platform
and mechanisms for spreading the gospel of Christ and for nurturing the
spiritual growth of those who are members of the community of believers.

---

42. This is not to say that there is no sense of monetary exchange within the church
setting. In a good number of cases, there is a small, paid staff while the vast majority are
volunteers who earn a living outside their church work.

43. 1 Timothy 6:10; Mark 11:15–17; Matthew 21:12; Luke 19:45.

44. Attention to the development of Black churches in urban areas during the Great
Migration points to the entrepreneurial dimension of the Black Church. See Best,
Passionately Human, No Less Divine, 153.

Second, work within the context of Black churches is labor for a business enterprise meant to advance both the spiritual and mundane missions of the corporation.

These two functions share a basic need met by women, who make up the vast majority of the Black Church's collective membership, namely labor and money. In a word, because of their numbers, women do most of the work in Black churches and thus represent a significant source of capital for these institutions.[45] Without women, Black churches could not financially support their missions and could not staff their various "teams" and working groups. "Yet any superficial observation of religion in contemporary society," Cheryl Townsend Gilkes argues, "will demonstrate that religious organizations contain within them structures and mechanisms which allocate power and authority. Religious systems are political systems, and very religious people can be quite political."[46] I would extend this to point out power dynamics and processes are not limited to the political realm. Rather, economic considerations inform the political and religious workings of churches rendering them, on some level, business enterprises.[47]

Perhaps we have been slow to consider theories of transformation and inclusion from the perspective of labor and finance in part because of what we have assumed concerning ties between labor movements and antireligion sentiments, although scholars such as Robin D. G. Kelle question the assumption of antireligious view points as a primary posture

---

45. The Pew Forum on Religion and Public Life on January 30, 2009, offered "A Religious Portrait of African Americans" that speaks to the religious devotion and numerical significance of Black women in religious communities. Sahgal and Smith, "A Religious Portrait of African Americans" (sections 1–3); Rasor and Chapman, *Black Power from the Pew*, 51.

46. Gilkes, "The Politics of 'Silence,'" 80.

47. The Black Church grows in size and strength during a period of intense economic and labor frustration for African Americans, a period when legal and extralegal avenues were used to control Black labor and to reduce the number of Blacks with economic strength through business and ownership of land. The economic growth of African Americans after the end of slavery challenged Whites and resulted in the structures of formal segregation. Black churches benefited from the economic development of Black communities and played some role in efforts to lessen the impact of segregation on African Americans. For information on the economic development of African American communities between Reconstruction and the rise of formal segregation see, for example, Moreno, *Black Americans and Organized Labor*.

within early twentieth century labor activism.[48] And more recent scholarship has softened the boundaries between church and organized labor by attempting to adjust perspectives on the antireligious concerns of figures such as labor leader A. Philip Randolph.[49] In addition, the assumption of incompatibility—the "it's not what the church does"—suggests a reason behind a notable failure, as Cornel West notes, to produce within the context of African American Christian thought and practice a solid social theory informed by figures such as Marx.[50] It is also possible that finance is not the basis of more conversation and consideration out of embarrassment in that some Black churches tend to manage poorly their money. "If the Black Church," Mamiya reflects, "has a major weakness, it is in the area of economics and finances. Black denominations need to be more concerned about the poor financial and membership record keeping in black churches."[51]

To call the church a business enterprise, again, does not render void its more spiritual and theologically expressed dimensions. It is not to ignore biblical warrants against obsessive relationships with money noted above. Instead, it is simply to recognize the mechanisms that in certain ways undergird the spiritual work of these churches.[52] Material acquisition, for instance, is present as an important theme from the very early signs of Black Church thought. Take for example the spirituals, one in particular: "I got shoes; you got shoes. All God's children got shoes to wear. When I get to heaven gonna put on my shoes and walk all over God's heaven." During another descriptive moment, listeners are informed that the streets

---

48. See Kelley, "'Comrades, Praise Gawd for Lenin and Them!'" It is worth noting that church leaders such as Reverdy Ransom and Richard R. Wright did weigh in on issues of labor and unions, but not necessarily in ways linked to the structures and orientations of Black churches. Furthermore, Martin Luther King Jr. and others within the civil rights movement gave attention to industrialization, unions, and economic development but concerns with mundane labor made little impact on the nature of church labor, and the manner in which Black women suffered as church workers.

49. Taylor, *A. Philip Randolph*.

50. West, *Prophesy Deliverance!*

51. Mamiya, *River of Struggle, River of Freedom*, 20.

52. Some might argue that such a take on the church desacralizes it in that I am pushing it into a class-based model of capitalism that ignores the moral and ethical principles deeply embedded in the workings of the Black Church tradition. I respond by arguing that Black churches do address issues of class, scholars have readily acknowledged this, as class issues are apparent in certain manifestation of church thought and practice. See Lawrence, *Reviving the Spirit*.

of heaven are paved with gold—a clear synergy between highly desired material goods and proper Christian conduct in that heaven is the reward for a life of devotion well lived. In some instances "wealth" might be rethought or spiritualized (e.g., rich in the gifts of the spirit, or rich in spiritual things), but a sense of acquisition, of gain, is not lost although it is tempered.[53]

Talk of Black churches as business enterprises does not do damage to moral and ethical principles as fundamental to the Black Church's *rasion d'être*.[54] Ethics figure into business dealings within this context as made clear from the rationale for stores, housing, and job training offered by churches such as First African Methodist Episcopal Church of Los Angeles ("FAME Church"), Windsor Village United Methodist Church in Houston, or Concord Baptist Church of Brooklyn, New York. For these churches and others like them, business development stems from a sense of good stewardship, whereby resources provided are to be properly grown in connection to an articulated requirement to provide for the needs of their communities.[55] Here a different emphasis marks the interpretation of the biblical warrant—"The Love of Money is the root of all evil"—in that acquisition of wealth for the sake of wealth—as an end in and of itself—is problematic. On the other hand, the possession and use of money as a means to an end is consistent with the will of God and the mission of the Black Church. To fail on this score—the use of wealth for the welfare of those in need—is to fail Christ:

---

53. What the appeal to goods in the spirituals suggests is historical and theological connection between the spiritual and the material within the context of Black Christianity. At times the relationship between the two lacks balance. For instance, what Gayraud Wilmore notes as the "re-radicalization" of the Black Church highlights a point in history (on going in some instances) during which the spiritual functions and interests of Black churches dwarfed regard for more material concerns. See Wilmore, *Black Religion and Black Radicalism*. Readers should also give attention to Sernett, *Bound for the Promised Land*.

54. And some might argue the prosperity gospel marks a contemporary turn in the other direction whereby material goods and class status become synonymous with (if not superceding) more clearly spiritual interests. For an example of this type of critique see: Franklin, "The Gospel Bling," 2007. For intriguing perspective on the prosperity gospel and megachurch phenomenon see Lee, *T. D. Jakes*; Lee and Sinitiere, *Holy Mavericks*; Harrison, *Righteous Riches*; Walton, *Watch This!*; Mitchem, *Name It and Claim It*.

55. R. Drew Smith, of Morehouse College's Leadership Center, has edited three volumes published with Duke University Press that provide interesting insights into the public engagement of Black churches, including attention to economic issues and entrepreneurial workings of Black churches.

For I was hungry, and ye did not give me to eat; I was thirsty, and ye gave me no drink; I was a stranger, and ye took me not in; naked, and ye clothed me not; sick, and in prison, and ye visited me not. Then shall they also answer, saying, Lord, when saw we thee hungry, or athirst, or a stranger, or naked, or sick, or in prison, and did not minister unto thee? Then shall he answer them, saying, verily I say unto you, inasmuch as ye did it not unto one of these least, ye did it not unto me.[56]

The question is not absence of moral and ethical standards but rather adherence to them. And, while Black churches outline certain moral and ethical principles as vital; the continuing discussion of its shortcomings with respect to discriminatory patterns would suggest spotty application of these principles. I do not reject the Black Church's sacred functions, but rather I realize that these sacred functions are supported in part through some rather mundane arrangements, commitments, procedures, and resources.[57] And, of great importance, women provide a noteworthy percentage of both labor and money that keep the Black Church tradition afloat.

Toward a New Protest Strategy

Numerous scholars point out the fundamental importance of women's participation in Black churches. According to Gilkes, "black women have remained committed to an institution that exists largely because of their extraordinary investments of time, talent, and economic resources . . . Black Women know how radically dependent their churches and communities are on their presence and actions for both organizational integrity and effective mobilization."[58] Recognition of the financial necessity of women to Black churches begs the question, why not push for real and meaningful change by withholding vital resources such as labor and money?

This question is particularly important if what Gilkes reports is true beyond the churches she observed: "The overwhelming female majorities in the early Sanctified Church meant that women's economic enterprise

---

56. Matthew 25:42–45.

57. This rationale for discussion of the business dimension of the Black churches was worked out through conversation with Cheryl Townsend Gilkes, Waterville, Maine, on February 9, 2009.

58. Gilkes, "*If It Wasn't for the Women . . .*," 7.

and labor force participation were essential for church growth and survival. Thus women's financial power was a major contradiction to the ethic
of male domination and control."[59] According to Gilkes, there are ways in
which this economic power prevented male leadership from short-circuit-
ing conversation related to issues uncomfortable to them, but it is also
clear that this economic power has not been used in ways that radically
change the very nature of power and the structures of authority available
to women. What seems to happen in these instances is the protection of
existing women's spheres of activity as seen through various auxiliaries,
but little more. Perhaps there are cracks in the walls of church patriarchy,
but these compromises do not seem to threaten in full the gender politics
of the Black Church as a general phenomenon. There may even be "shared"
power, but this is far from a situation of equity and this "sharing" of power
does not create equal opportunity based on talent.[60] Only organizational
and ideological disruption caused through the withholding of resources
such as money and labor can result in sustained change.[61]

There has been a general failure to note the importance of this de-
pendence on women as the basis for protest leading to long-term and far-
reaching change within Black churches: withhold the significant resources
offered by women—labor and money—and Black churches will be forced
to change their practices with regard to the requirements for professional
ministry and leadership roles. Churches do not want to close; they want
to maintain their viability and relevance, and they will make changes to
accomplish this.[62]

It is possible that some ministers and some laity will hold to sexist
practices and will allow their churches to close their doors before they
will change their practices. I believe it is safe to say, however, that these
churches are in the minority and are likely already suffering due to a similar rigidity regarding other issues. By and large, churches will respond in

---

59. Gilkes, "*If It Wasn't for the Women . . .* ," 53.

60. Ibid.

61. The civil rights movement serves as a prime example of the manner in which disruption produces sought after change. See, for example, Morris and Clawson, "Lessons of
the Civil Rights Movement for Building a Worker Rights Movement."

62. For example, resistance to gospel music was initially strong within many circles
but the financial possibilities generated by gospel—increased church attendance, increased revenue and prestige—resulted in the eventual acceptance of this musical form.
What is more, biblical arguments and theological rhetoric regarding gospel music shifted
to fit and explain this new embrace. See Michael W. Harris, *The Rise of Gospel Blues.*

ways meant to safeguard their health and vitality, and this will mean meeting the needs of Black women seeking greater leadership opportunities.

It is important to note that the strategy I propose is not foreign. Rather it involves a shift in conceptualization of the church and use on the collective level of what has been an approach by individuals. Put differently, there is a tradition of Black women withholding money, or at times their presence, due to disagreement with the pastor on a variety of issues. This has been a matter of personal disassociation, however, as opposed to a corporate and organized means of group protest. As was the case with some of the church mothers who left my home church during my youth for extended periods, they were missed; but their departure did not cause the type of dissonance that would result in fundamental change to the manner in which my home church operated. The church "rolled on," and they eventually came back, or found other church homes.

Reverend Dr. Pauli Murray, the first African American woman ordained as an Episcopal priest also exercised this option. She reasoned her discontent with the sexism of her denomination along with its less than inspired response to racial discrimination could only be addressed by her departure from the Church. Although Murray's story is not connected to one of the major Black denomination, the general nature of her protest is instructive:

> These innovations [small gains in lay ministry roles] only whetted my desire to help do away with other restrictions, for they served to emphasize the male domination of the most elaborate and solemn serves of the week—the Holy Eucharist on Sunday morning . . .
>
> I do not know why this familiar spectacle suddenly became intolerable to me one Sunday morning in March 1966 . . . I remember only that in the middle of the celebration of the Holy Eucharist an uncontrollable anger exploded inside me, filling me with such rage I had to get up and leave. I wandered about the streets full of blasphemous thought, feeling alienated from God . . . If the present church customs were justified then I did not belong in the church and it became a stumbling block to faith.[63]

It seems there was little notice to this outside her circle of friends and the readers of her autobiographical writings. Murray eventually returned and pressed for radical change from within the denomination and in

---

63. Murray, *Song in a Weary Throat*, 370. Quoted in Pinn, *Becoming "America's Problem Child,"* 36.

cooperation with likeminded women and men.[64] The time apart provided an opportunity for perspective, to assess and contextualize her demands, but the achieving of her concerns required more than the resolve and actions of an individual in isolation. This type of organizing for change is of limited consequence.

Furthermore, when seeking a role in ordained ministry denied them explicitly on the basis of gender, some women leave their home church for affiliation with independent churches or denominations more welcoming of their sense of calling and preferred arenas of service. While these churches are far from problem free, one must note the importance of "sanctified churches" for women seeking ministerial opportunities in that these churches gave more importance to demonstrated holiness over gender as the test of "calling" and the right to exercise church authority. However, the strong reliance on the authority of Scripture, often based on a literalist interpretation, limits the ability of these churches to pose a challenge to structures of discrimination beyond offering a somewhat "safe haven."[65]

Movement to more supportive churches increased the presence of women within contexts already welcoming, but this does not result as far as I can tell in a fundamental change in the policies of churches opposed to gender equality on all levels. Useful on some level, yet since this modality of protest ultimately is not organized, systematic, and possessive of regularized impact. Missing from this approach is a targeted attack on structures of discrimination by women as the offended and aggrieved parties (and male supporters) and requiring redress by discriminators.

The challenge to gender-based discrimination in church work requires the organized insistence marked by efforts such as the National Association of Colored Women that fought for the socioeconomic and political needs of Black women. This organization displayed the power of collective action. As Mary Eliza Church Terrell reflects,

> But it dawned upon them finally, that individuals working alone,
> or scattered here and there in small companies, might be ever
> so honest in purpose, so indefatigable in labor, so conscientious

---

64. Murray, *Song in a Weary Throat*; Pinn, ed., *Pauli Murray*; and Pinn, *Becoming "America's Problem Child."* Readers may also be interested in the Pauli Murray Papers, located at the Schlesinger Library at Harvard University.

65. See, for example: Mamiya, *River of Struggle, River of Freedom*; Best, *Passionately Human, No Less Divine*; and Wiggins, *Righteous Content*.

about methods, and so wise in projecting plans, yet they would accomplish little, compared with the possible achievement of many individuals, all banded together throughout the entire land, with heads and hearts fixed on the same high purpose and hands joined in united strength. As a result of a general realization of this fact, the national Association of Colored Women was born.[66]

There is little advantage to arguing over the destructive practices of many Black churches. Instead, Black women (and supportive Black men) might let their feet do the talking—leave and take their money with them until churches begin a process of significant change. The strategy is as follows:

1. reconceptualize work that moves away from a spiritual economy and labor as spiritual practice;

2. move away from theo-biblical refutation of discrimination;

3. utilize denomination-wide organizations as platforms for collective action;

4. articulate clear objectives and goals; and

5. strike!

Such a strategy might produce positive outcomes regardless of the organizational structure of a particular denomination or the availability of nonordained modalities of church involvement open to women.[67]

As Daphne C. Wiggins notes, there is a commitment to family and relationships that guides much (if not all) of what happens within Black churches, and this commitment begins early when children are required to attend services as part of their familial and individual development and socialization. This imprinting on young Black girls, Wiggins asserts, enforces the importance of the church as a dimension of the well-rounded life and also projects it as "female-friendly."[68] While agreeing with this,

66. Riggs, *Can I Get a Witness?* 69–70.

67. This approach to protest is in its early stages, and I will need to do additional work on this topic, including thinking through this strategy in light of social-movement theory. The purpose of this chapter, however, is simply to point in the direction of a new possibility for effective protest and to begin outlining the rationale for using it as well as its basic structure.

68. Wiggins, *Righteous Content*, 20–31. I must, as Wiggins points out, acknowledge the efforts of groups such as Sisters Working Encouraging Empowering Together (Denver) for their efforts on issues related to women in the church. This organization, however, attempts to create more space for women within the existing system. What I seek is a fundamental troubling of that system in ways that necessitate structural change.

I would argue the approach I am suggesting accounts for the layered nature of women's participation in Black churches (both in and outside mainline traditions), but reframes and reorganizes connections and relationships beyond family lines to include the connections of commitment and equality that guide the quest for equality. By so doing, I promote an implicit and explicit challenge to the normalization of discrimination likely to take place during early church-based socialization. Collective action as argued here simply extends the shape and content of relationships as a guiding arrangement in churches.[69] Furthermore, what I propose is consistent with Gilkes's notion of "community work" in that this stepping away from injustice in the form of gender-restricted access to church participation "consists of everything that people do to address oppression in their own lives, suffering in the lives of others, and their sense of solidarity or group kinship."[70]

However, in outlining the compatibility of the strategy I suggest with notions of relationship and church family is not meant to gloss over problems with the family model. To the contrary, problems with a family model abound in that it typically assumes the traditional nuclear family and reads this through a conservative ideology, which posits the special authority of the father (hence male leadership in the church and perhaps the assumed maleness of God) and the normative status of the heterosexual. So arranged, both heterosexism and patriarchy are supported and given an integrity difficult to challenge. Within my model of protest, familial relationship (spiritual or biological) lodged in churches are challenged to the extent they support inequality; when this is the case the demand for accountability and opportunity challenges the moral authority of relationships that in effect undermine the value and opportunities of its participants.

Protest meant to rethink the scope of and criteria for participation in the once male-dominated arenas of church involvement does not destroy the workings of relationships at their best, but rather challenges the integrity of relationships based on gender bias. On this point I am not suggesting that solidarity has not been a mark of women's activism within churches; rather, I argue solidarity has held as its organizing logic an un-

---

69. I am indebted to Cheryl Townsend Gilkes for the wonderful insights and critique she provided during a conversation in Waterville, Maine, on February 9, 2009. That conversation has improved my attention to numerous dimensions of my argument.

70. Gilkes, "If It Wasn't for the Women . . . ," 17.

productive structure (e.g., traditional nuclear family ideology) which has meant little Black Church-wide gain for women.

Finally, what I propose as a more robust strategy for promoting change does not necessarily result in changed personal preference; instead it works to prevent personal levels of comfort from harming the leadership options available to women.[71] Some resentment will be expressed undoubtedly through the departure of members unwilling to negotiate. This is unavoidable; but, because of the multiple functions of churches, it is important to address and implement explicitly efforts to minimize resentment. The therapeutic function of Black churches (revolving, for example, around group prayer and counseling) provides existing and easily tapped mechanisms for working through reactions of resentment. But, even if some protest change, leave and don't return, if they decided to take other paths . . . Let the church roll on!

---

71. I model this on Derek Bell's response to racial preference discussed in *Faces at the Bottom of the Well.*

Concluding Thoughts

New Possibilities for the Black Church[1]

I END THIS BOOK by marking out the beginning of new religious possibilities, new opportunities for Black churches to re-access and rethink their relationship to the fundamental claims of this country and their place in the public arena—all made possible through a political development that has been long awaited.

To be sure, the election of President Barack Obama marked a major shift in United States politics, but also offered an opportunity to think about the role of religion in public affairs. It was clear throughout the campaign that less is known about the Black Church tradition than one might anticipate, particularly in light of the civil rights struggle and the role of some prominent churches and ministers in that struggle.

Little is known about these churches in spite of the continued assumption that Black churches are the lifeblood of Black communities and collectively serve as one of the nation's more important moral compasses. Much of this misunderstanding and general lack of information concerning Black churches surfaced in the debate concerning President Obama's relationship to Rev. Jeremiah Wright. While the use of this debate as a political "football" has subsided, the need to think through that development as a way of framing an ongoing conversation concerning the relationship between Black churches and the political process continues.

There is no doubt that our country has known more than its share of political tension wed to religious fervor. From the first movement of Europeans across the great ocean, to the destruction of indigenous cultures and the enslavement of Africans, to our discomfort with the residue

---

1. This essay was first published in three parts: "Getting Wright Wrong: Preaching Is Not Policy," *Religion Dispatches* (April 3, 2008); "Inauguration Day: Re-imagining Ourselves," *Religion Dispatches* (January 20, 2009); and "O(Pinn)ion: Reevaluating a Faith-Based Nation," *Religion Dispatches* (February 13, 2009)

of such situations, our sociopolitical, economic and cultural geography has been mapped in relationship to our religious leanings and assumptions. From then until now, religious commitment and religious informed political opinions have wrestled with the pressing issues of the day. Popular imagination and public debate, surrounding President Obama's former pastor, Rev. Jeremiah Wright, has highlighted the manner in which the Black Church tradition plays into religious engagement of political concerns in the United States. I do not lament this debate, but I do regret the rather limited scope of the conversation, the way in which what is really a long and robust tradition of critique and celebration of the United States in Black churches has been reduced to a few inflammatory sound-bites.

Beginning with the emergence of the spirituals, people of African descent applied scriptural lessons to their daily concerns and social predicament. Through a merging of scriptural moral and ethical principles drawn from biblical characters like Moses and Daniel with their experience of oppression, they expressed their hope for a better life. This reading of life through the Bible allowed slaves to sing, "Didn't my Lord deliver Daniel, and why not everyone?" and it provided the framework and language for struggle against oppressive circumstances writ large. As the Christian thought and practice of enslaved Africans grew into visible churches, this evaluation of life arrangements through the insights and principles of scripture continued.

This mode of expression included not just song but the Black sermonic style. From the First Great Awakening in the 1730s on, enslaved Africans and free Africans preached the word of God in revivals, camp meetings, and pulpits. By the 1800s, in some cases they gave these sermons from pulpits within their own churches and within local congregations associated with Black denominations. From pulpits across the land, ministers spoke to the pressing issues of the day in light of the unchanging truths of the gospel message. Some churches, of course, moved in a direction that is commonly called an "other-worldly" orientation through which the priority in preaching and practice revolved around personal salvation and little sustained attention was given to social activism—a posture against the world. Others, however, representing the more celebrated approach, advanced a "this-worldly" orientation, using the preached moment as an opportunity to advance life options that diminished racism. What they preached was the social gospel associated with figures such as

Walter Rauschenbusch—the scripture-based assumption that Christian commitment *requires* social activism.[2]

There is nothing distant and disinterested about the Black sermonic style, but rather it utilizes body movement, shifts in tone, to push the urgency of the theme. And this dynamic approach to the preached word is often combined with language meant to demonstrate the sustained importance of the topic. At times this language is inflammatory, radical, demanding. Yes, this can involve a critique of the United States, a critique of its shortcomings, its failure to live up to its democratic principles and religious rhetoric. Without this type of critique, for example, we don't have the Holiness Movement and we don't have the civil rights movement.

We found out just how inflammatory, how challenging, this language can be when small segments of a few of Rev. Jeremiah Wright's sermons hit "YouTube" and national television programs. The question was raised ad nauseam by numerous figures: How can [then] Senator Obama maintain membership in a church whose (former) minister would say such things about the country? There is no doubt that some of Rev. Wright's comments are inflammatory—yes, yes, yes, inflammatory. Yet, do we gain a full sense of his thirty-plus-year ministry through a few statements taken from his sermons? Yes, the statements were inflammatory, but one should not read this as suggesting inflammatory as denoted necessarily negative. Rather, in the midst of our complacency, inflammatory as I am using it refers to things uncomfortable to hear and challenging of basic assumptions.

If one imagines that his sermons probably average thirty minutes in length, what do we learn from a thirty-second or even a three-minute clip? What of the better than sixty outreach ministries found at Trinity United Church of Christ? Do they speak to hopelessness, defeatism, and "un-American" attitudes? What do they tell us about Rev. Wright's take on the gospel message, his commitment to the improvement of life in the United States? His deep disappointment with the failures of the United States is connected to a profound hopefulness that the moral and ethical principles that have served to frame our country can be enlivened, and both are presented in passionate language not dissimilar from that used by Hebrew Bible prophets such as the reverend's namesake, Jeremiah. Rev. Wright's sense of ministry, his read of the Bible, when placed in

2. Rauschenbusch, *Christianity and the Social Crisis*; Rasuchenbusch, *A Theology for the Social Gospel.*

context extends beyond a few questionable comments and speaks to the social gospel representing the best of the Christian tradition in the United States, and the benchmark of the Black Church tradition.

It should not be forgotten that underlying Rev. Wright's message is a concern with a fundamental problem in the United States, one as old as the nation itself: Racism. (Worthy of some conversation, and noted elsewhere in this book, is a failure to speak in substantive ways to the manner in which both racism and sexism, for instance, impact the life circumstances of Black women who make up the bulk of Black Church membership in the United States.) But one must remember that preaching is neither public policy nor political campaigning, *and* that Rev. Wright was not running for the presidency of the United States.

Outside of political maneuvering, it is difficult to understand the assumption that Rev. Wright's commentary somehow represents and reflects President Obama's religious commitments and religious thought. Such a misguided notion fails to recognize the nature of church membership, which is based on a shared and very general posture toward the world, shared values and vision premised on the church's praxis. Church membership does not require complete agreement with every sociopolitical (or theological) pronouncement made by the pastor. Is it really reasonable to believe every member of every church is in full agreement with the pastor on all issues at all times? Such a requirement would result in empty churches across the country.

President Obama was clear in the Philadelphia "Race" speech: He rejects what he considers conversation that is divisive, language that does not encourage the best of our democratic principles, and does not embrace our highest moral and ethical values. However, he embraced Trinity Church's commitment to the social gospel, and he does so in a robust manner. It isn't clear to me, however, that President Obama is an advocate of Black liberation theology—as Rev. Wright is—as opposed to a more general embrace of liberal religion's emphasis on active faith. President Obama's theological perspective seems to echo the sensitivity and the deep yearning for meaning and community of Howard Thurman, the religious realism of Reinhold Niebuhr, the religious engagement of sociopolitical life of Benjamin Mays, and the "beloved community" longed for by Martin Luther King Jr. And, unlike many African American ministers and professional writers of Black theology, President Obama attempts to speak to an appreciation for religious pluralism in the United States, the merit of difference, and a shared moral and ethical standard that cuts across religious traditions.

Democracy requires sustained, rigorous, and public conversation, concerning moral and ethical principles and political vision—but it must involve more than just sound bites and political slogans. What this public conversation must involve is rather obvious. First, this conversation must be based on the recognition that critique of the United States is not synonymous with unpatriotic ranting, nor is it of necessity a sign of hate. To the contrary, passionate critique of the United States is a sign of patriotism, in that it arises from a deep need to push the country to be the best it can be, to embrace its full potential and live out its principles. In this public conversation, we must be open to hearing diverse perspectives and opinions. These differences must be respected and allowed to shape healthy and rich exchange through which we learn a great deal about the texture of our nation and appreciate the diversity of thought and practice—religious and otherwise—that has marked the United States from its very origin. Public debate of this kind is tough, often uncomfortable, and bound to expose both the best of our praxis and the worst of our inclinations.[3]

Next this conversation must entail more than a jockeying for political advantage. As hard as this might be, our public conversation must attend to the reshaping of the nation's posture toward its citizens and the world—an issue larger than which political party controls key offices. Rather it has to do with the self-perception of our country and the manner in which this self-perception reflects high values and honest dealings. It is also important that this debate be based on a solid sense of our history, the events and practices that have shaped our current condition. Too often we engage in dialogue based on a romanticized sense of our past, a chronicling of our internal and external dealings devoid of the more nasty moments and embarrassing activities. While this might make us feel better, it does not allow us to really address our shortcomings and celebrate our success in ways that will promote our growth as a nation and as a member of the larger world community.

Public debate and dialogue that allows us to reach the heights of our potential and to tap the depths of our best selves must be mature. By that I mean it must reflect who we are as a people and must note those things that keep us from being all we should be. To use religious language,

---

3. See West, *Race Matters*.

there is something confessional about this process, a matter of purging and repenting for the ways in which we have failed ourselves; but, it also connotes humble acknowledgment of things well done, all framed by a commitment to do an even better job of living out of a shared moral and ethical vision of collective life. And perhaps the historic events of November 4, 2008, marked a particularly encouraging sign of our prog-ress as a country, a sign that we are in fact on the very edge of a prom-ise exemplified by a committed to honest debate and the production of healthy life options for all.

Although we must proceed with caution, guided by measured op-timism and a mature realism, it is impossible to deny the significance of what citizens of the United States achieved on November 4, 2008, with unquestionable clarity. We, as a nation, have moved that much closer to re-envisioning the nature and meaning of our democratic ideals in ways that prioritize our values, our ethical commitments, over against the look of our bodies. In this sense, we have made important strides towards liv-ing the best of our principles by pushing toward confrontation with an embarrassing past marked by exclusion.

We must recognize, however, that oppression is web-like in nature, a series of interrelated modalities of exclusion. We cannot allow individual victories to blind us to the ongoing forms of discrimination. Voters on November 4, 2008, called for new ways of doing things, new understand-ings of our diversity as creative possibility. This points in the direction of our potential for transformative actions. But, as religious scholar Reinhold Niebuhr reminded his contemporaries during the twentieth century, humans are also prone to great evil: Our transformation of life options in sustained ways, prolonged push to the good achieved in light of the best of our deep commitments, is a delicate operation destroyed so very easily.

Therefore, we do extreme damage if we assume the election of Barack Obama marked the end of struggle. No, it places our country on the edge of a promise. It is an opportunity uncovered, not an opportunity fulfilled. This statement is not meant to take away from the historic nature of the achievement we have made for ourselves, and the world. Rather, it is meant to suggest the need for a measured realism—recognition that this does not signal the death note of racism, sexism, classism, homophobia, and the other modalities of injustice that have infected our nation.

Instead, those millions of votes for Obama pointed out determination to foster change, to enhance life options, to re-imagine the nature and look of life in these United States. What is interesting is the manner in which Obama points to the failure of race politics as the shape of this reimagining. Oppression remains a target of attack, but racial discrimination is placed within a larger context and subordinated to a more fundamental call for change. It is a twenty-first-century return to Martin Luther King Jr.'s call for the "content of character" as the final marker of our being.

As scholars remind us, the "reading" of bodies in ways that support White supremacy marks much of our history. Through what Cornel West refers to as the "normative gaze," White bodies were "read" or viewed as markers of beauty, intellect and ability; while Black, Brown, and Red bodies were viewed as being of less importance, less beautiful and therefore available for the benefit of White Americans. The 2008 presidential election cracked this process, exposed its flaws, and just might have encouraged a different take on bodies once despised. Black bodies, bodies like President Obama's, can no longer be so easily assumed dangerous, odd, or "other" in a negative manner. Or can they?

Current events mark much needed dissonance between the problematic assumptions that have lurked behind our ideological postures and political processes, and the real importance and promise of our diversity. And so, the election of President Obama does not simply signal response to economic crisis. There is something more fundamental taking place— a desire to reimagine ourselves, to reshape ourselves on a economic and political level; but more importantly on the level of our basic purpose as a people, on the level of concerns and commitments that shape us existentially and ontologically—shape us in terms of our historical existence and the nature and meaning of our very being.

The promise marked by this new political environment, if we embrace it, will shake us to our foundation and force us to be more than we have been, to live in light of our higher ideals. This hopefulness, however, must be tempered in that it is all too easy to return to the easy patterns of life, the old and worn markers of interaction as conflict. Perhaps the election of Obama in years to come will encourage children to see expansive possibilities for themselves; but only hard work can provide the opportunity for achieving those dreams.

What we achieved on November 4, 2008, marks an appreciation for those who have struggled for the best of this country's potential. It is an embrace of their hope and a commitment to the legacy of their struggle. This shift in our politics requires recognition of "change" as necessary and as a fundamental part of what is best about our democratic ideals. It requires something of a leap of faith by supporting a relatively new political figure, and it required a willingness to avoid the easy political rhetoric, and demand more of our nation. But there is more ahead of us. We have not fully recognized and exorcised the worst of our inclinations and patterns of behavior. We have not embraced in full the problems we must address, the problems we have created. That type of awakening and praxis entails more than the casting of a vote.

From the president we have also received a vision of religious diversity and pluralism not often voiced within political circles. And for many Black Christians this may be difficult to stomach. While Christianity remains prominent in the vocabulary and grammar of U.S. democracy, he has acknowledged valuable albeit competing faith claims. During his inaugural address, President Obama included the mention of nonbelief in the litany of perspectives that must be recognized and respected. This sign of inclusion sparked a range of responses, with a good number of "nonbelievers" expressing appreciation for President Obama's openness to a philosophy of life often held suspect.

On the surface, his remark was a welcomed effort to counter popular imagination and, to remap the religious landscape of the United States. However, it served to raise more questions than it answered: What is the real look of this inclusion? What are substantive signs of this inclusion? If all these various traditions are given equal footing in the public arena, in spite of their profound differences, what exactly is religion? If there is no clear distinction between the "sacred" and the "secular," how does one define religion anew? How does one recognize and respond to "religiously" motivated opinions and practices?

These are important but frustrated questions when one keeps in mind, for example, the context in which the President spoke his words: The theistic tone of the inauguration framed as it was by prayers to the Christian God. The effort to speak to those who do not embrace theistic claims and orientations is appreciated; but it is muffled by Christian vocabulary and grammar that serves in an unquestioned fashion to awkwardly outline this tolerance.

Overcoming this dilemma must involve more than making certain to better equip more religious communities for service. That is, a reconceived Faith Based and Neighborhood Partnership Office is not enough. What I am suggesting here is too big a job for the Office of Faith Based and Neighborhood Partnerships—too important for the occasional breakfast meeting or quick information session.

A more inclusive approach to which religious organizations receive money and the types of issues that can be addressed using this money is a push beyond what we encountered in the Bush Administration. And it is encouraging for President Obama to say this Faith Based and Neighborhood Partnership Office "will not be to favor one religious group over another—or even religious groups over secular groups. It will simply be to work on behalf of those organizations that want to work on behalf of our communities, and to do so without blurring the line our founders wisely drew between church and state."[4]

But the more difficult task involves development of the national posture necessary for achieving this vision. The problem is obvious, religious traditions involve competing faith claims, conflicting postures toward the practice of faith, and shifting assumptions concerning the public nature of religious commitment. Rich, "thick," and complex discourse requires new structures and consequently, new rules of engagement—a push beyond what marks the current and public framing of religious concerns and practices. Great care must be exercised, or what we will get is superficial tolerance of religious Humanists and secularists, a sense of what it means to be religious in the United States that barely hides an assumed theistic, if not Christian, backstory.

President Obama's call for recognition of religious diversity falls short in that little thus far suggests this appeal entails a fundamental re-thinking of how we in the United States define, arrange, and shape our fundamental concerns. There is an opportunity here that should not be missed. Rather than simply assuming there is a clear understanding of what it means to be "American" and "religious," here is a chance to inter-rogate the wide range of possibilities. This involves sustained examina-tion of what it means—and what must be surrendered—to embrace all modalities of religion within the context of this democracy.

---

4. This quotation is from President Obama's speech at the National Prayer Breakfast, Washington DC on February 5, 2009. Onine: http://www.usnews.com/blogs/god-and-country/2009/02/05/president-barack-obamas-speech-at-national-prayer-breakfast.html/.

The signs of a morally and ethically centered and successful nation might need some rethinking in light of the various (and, at times, competing) norms held dear and celebrated within the context of our religious diversity. Black churches most certainly are a part of this process, but this celebrated diversity will require African American Christians to rethink themselves and their institutions and ultimately act in ways that are mindful of this pluralism. Developing ways to accomplish this tactic is perhaps one of the Black Church's next big challenges, one that amounts to an ongoing task.

Bibliography

Allen, Norm R., Jr., editor. *African American Humanism: An Anthology*. Buffalo: Prometheus, 1991.

———. *The Black Humanist Experience: An Alternative to Religion*. Buffalo: Prometheus, 2002.

Altizer, Thomas J. J., and William Hamilton. *Radical Theology and the Death of God*. Indianapolis: Bobbs-Merrill, 1966.

Anderson, Victor. *Beyond Ontological Blackness: An Essay on African American Religious and Cultural Criticism*. New York: Continuum, 1995.

———. *Creative Exchange: A Constructive Theology of African American Religious Experience*. Innovations. Minneapolis: Fortress, 2008.

Andrews, Dale. *Practical Theology for Black Churches: Bridging Black Theology and African American Folk Religion*. Louisville: Westminster John Knox, 2002.

Baldwin, Lewis V. *There Is a Balm in Gilead: The Cultural Roots of Martin Luther King, Jr.* Minneapolis: Fortress, 1991.

Barnes, Sandra L. "Black Church Culture and Community Action." *Social Forces* 84 (2005) 967–94.

———. "Whosoever Will Let Her Come: Social Activism and Gender Inclusivity in the Black Church." *Journal for the Scientific Study of Religion* 45 (2006) 371–87.

Bell, Derek A. *Faces at the Bottom of the Well: The Permanence of Racism*. New York BasicBooks, 1993.

———. *Silent Covenants: Brown v. Board of Education and the Unfulfilled Hopes for Racial Reform*. New York: Oxford University Press, 2005.

Berlin, Ira et al., editors. *Remembering Slavery: African Americans Talk About Their Personal Experiences of Slavery and Emancipation*. New York: New Press, 1998.

Best, Wallace D. *Passionately Human, No Less Divine: Religion and Culture in Black Chicago, 1915–1952*. Princeton: Princeton University Press, 2005.

Billingsley, Andrew. *Mighty Like a River: The Black Church and Social Reform*. New York: Oxford University Press, 2003.

Billson, Janet Mancini. "No Owner of Soil: Redefining the Concept of Marginality." In *Marginality, Power, and Social Structure: Issues in Race, Class, and Gender Analysis*, edited by Rutledge M. Dennis, 29–48. Research in Race and Ethnic Relations 12. New York: Elsevier, 2005.

Burrows, Rufus, Jr. *God and Human Dignity: The Personalism, Theology, and Ethics of Martin Luther King, Jr.* Notre Dame: University of Notre Dame Press, 2006.

———. "Personalism, the Objective Moral Order, and Moral Law in the Work of Martin Luther King, Jr." In *The Legacy of Martin Luther King, Jr.: The Boundaries of Law, Politics, and Religion*, edited by Lewis V. Baldwin, et al., 213–51. Notre Dame: University of Notre Dame Press, 2002.

Callahan, Allen Dwight. *The Talking Book: African Americans and the Bible*. New Haven: Yale University Press, 2006.

Carson, Clayborne. "Martin Luther King, Jr., and the African-American Social Gospel." In *African American Christianity: Essays in History*, edited by Paul E. Johnson, 159–78. Berkeley: University of California Press, 1994.

Chatters, Linda M., et al. "African American Religious Participation: A Multi-Sample Comparison." *Journal for the Scientific Study of Religion* 38 (1999) 132–45.

Chesebrough, David B. *"God Ordained This War": Sermons on the Sectional Crisis, 1830–1865*. Columbia: University of South Carolina Press, 1991.

Cobble, Dorothy Sue. "Introduction." In *The Sex of Class: Women Transforming American Labor*, edited by Dorothy Sue Cobble, 1–12. Ithaca: ILR Press, 2007.

Collier-Thomas, Bettye, editor. *Daughters of Thunder: Black Women Preachers and Their Sermons, 1850–1979*. San Francisco: Jossey-Bass, 1998.

Cone, James H. *A Black Theology of Liberation*. 20th anniversary ed. Maryknoll, NY: Orbis, 1990.

———. *For My People: Black Theology and the Black Church*. The Bishop Henry McNeal Turner Studies in North American Black Religion 1. Maryknoll, NY: Orbis, 1984.

———. *God of the Oppressed*. New York: Seabury, 1975.

Cone, James H., and Gayraud S. Wilmore, editors. *Black Theology: A Documentary History*. 2 vols. 2nd rev. ed. Maryknoll, NY: Orbis, 1993.

Crummell, Alexander. *Destiny and Race: Selected Writings, 1840–1898*. Edited with an introduction by Wilson Jeremiah Moses. Amherst: University of Massachusetts Press, 1992.

Díaz, Miguel H. *On Being Human: U.S. Hispanic and Rahnerian Perspectives*. Faith and Cultures Series. Maryknoll, NY: Orbis, 2001.

Dixon, Thomas. *The Clansman: An Historical Romance of the Ku Klux Klan*. Illustrated by Arthur I. Keller. Ridgewood, NJ: Gregg, 1967.

"The Doctrine of the Church of God in Christ." Online: http://www.cogic.com/doctrine.html/

Dorrien, Gary. *The Making of American Liberal Theology: Crisis, Irony, and Postmodernity, 1950–2005*. Louisville: Westminster John Knox, 2006.

Douglas, Kelly Brown. *The Black Christ*. The Bishop Henry McNeal Turner Studies in North American Black Religion 9. Maryknoll, NY: Orbis, 1994.

———. *Sexuality and the Black Church: A Womanist Perspective*. Minneapolis: Fortress, 1999.

———. *What's Faith Got to Do With It? Black Bodies/Christian Souls*. Maryknoll, NY: Orbis, 2005.

Douglas, Mary. *Natural Symbols: Explorations in Cosmology*, with a new introduction. New York: Routledge, 1996.

Ellison, Christopher G. "Are Religious People Nice People? Evidence from the National Survey of Black Americans." *Social Forces* 71 (1992) 411–30.

Ellwood, Robert S. *The Sixties Spiritual Awakening: American Religion Moving from Modern to Postmodern*. New Brunswick, NJ: Rutgers University Press, 1994.

Evans, James H., Jr. *We Have Been Believers: An African-American Systematic Theology*. Minneapolis: Fortress, 1992.

Fanon, Frantz. *Black Skin, White Masks*. New York: Grove, 1967.

Fauset, Arthur Huff. *Black Gods of the Metropolis: Negro Religious Cults of the Urban North*. Philadelphia: University of Pennsylvania Press, 1971.

Featherstone, Mike et al., editors. *The Body: Social Process and Cultural Theory*. Theory, Culture & Society. London: Sage, 2001.

Foreman, James. "God Is Dead: A Question of Power." In *By These Hands: A Documentary History of African American Humanism*, edited by Anthony B. Pinn, 269–85. New York: New York University Press, 2001.

Franklin, Robert M. "The Gospel Bling." *Sojourners* 36 (2007) 18.

Gates, Henry Lewis, Jr. "The Face and Voice of Blackness." In *Facing History: The Black Image in American Art 1710–1940*, edited by Guy C. McElroy, xxix–xix. San Francisco: Bedford Arts, 1990.

Gilgoff, Dan. "President Barack Obama's Remarks at the National Prayer Breakfast. God & Country." *U.S. News and World Report*. Online: http://www.usnews.com/blogs/god-and-country/2009/02/05/president-barack-obamas-speech-at-national-prayer-breakfast.html/.

Gilkes, Cheryl Townsend. *"If It Wasn't for the Women . . .": Black Women's Experience and Womanist Culture in Church and Community*. Maryknoll, NY: Orbis, 2000.

———. "The Politics of 'Silence': Dual-Sex Political Systems and Women's Traditions of Conflict in African-American Religion," 80–110. In *African American Christianity: Essays in History*, edited by Paul E. Johnson. Berkeley: University of California Press, 1994.

Girard, René. *Things Hidden since the Foundation of the World*. Translated by Stephen Bann and Michael Metteer. Stanford: Stanford University Press, 1987.

———. *Violence and the Sacred*. Translated by Patrick Gregory. Baltimore: The Johns Hopkins University Press, 1977.

Glaude, Eddie S., Jr. *Exodus! Religion, Race, and Nation in Early Nineteenth-Century Black America*. Chicago: University of Chicago Press, 2000.

Goatley, David Emmanuel. *Were You There? Godforsakeness in Slave Religion*. The Bishop Henry McNeal Turner/Sojourner Truth Series in Black Religion 11. Maryknoll, NY: Orbis, 1996.

Gomez, Michael A. *Reversing Sail: A History of the African Diaspora*. New Approaches to African History. Cambridge: Cambridge University Press, 2004.

Grant, Jacquelyn. *White Women's Christ and Black Women's Jesus: Feminist Christology and Womanist Response*. American Academy of Religion Academy Series 64. Atlanta: Scholars, 1989.

Hall, John R. "Peoples Temple." In *America's Alternative Religions*, edited by Timothy Miller, 301–11. SUNY Series in Religious Studies. Albany: State University of New York Press, 1995.

Hall, Stuart. "Cultural Studies: Two Paradigms." *Media, Culture and Society* 2 (1980) 57–72.

———. "What is This 'Black' in Black Popular Culture?" In *Black Popular Culture*, a project of Michele Wallace, edited by Gina Dent, 21–33. Discussions in Contemporary Culture 8. New York: New Press, 1998.

Harris, Fredrick C. *Something Within: Religion in African-American Political Activism*. New York: Oxford University Press, 1999.

Harris, Michael D. *Colored Pictures: Race and Visual Representation*. Chapel Hill: University of North Carolina Press, 2003.

Harris, Michael W. *The Rise of Gospel Blues: The Music of Thomas Andrew Dorsey in the Urban Church*. New York: Oxford University Press, 1994.

Harrison, Milmon F. *Righteous Riches: The Word of Faith Movement in Contemporary African American Religion*. New York: Oxford University Press, 2005.

Hayes, Diana L. *Hagar's Daughters: Womanist Ways of Being in the World.* Madeleva Lecture in Spirituality 1995. New York: Paulist, 1995.

Higginbotham, Evelyn Brooks. *Righteous Discontent: The Women's Movement in the Black Baptist Church, 1880–1920.* Cambridge: Harvard University Press, 1993.

Hill, Johnny Bernard. *The Theology of Martin Luther King, Jr. and Desmond Mpilo Tutu.* Black Religion, Womanist Thought, Social Justice. New York: Palgrave Macmillan, 2007.

hooks, bell. *Feminist Theory: From Margin to Center.* Boston: South End, 1984.

Hopkins, Dwight N. *Being Human: Race, Culture, and Religion.* Minneapolis: Fortress, 2005.

———. *Down, Up, and Over: Slave Religion and Black Theology.* Minneapolis: Fortress, 1999.

———. *Introducing Black Theology of Liberation.* Maryknoll, NY: Orbis, 1999.

———. "Introduction: Black Faith and Public Talk." In *Black Faith and Public Talk: Critical Essays on James H. Cone's "Black Theology and Black Power,"* edited by Dwight N. Hopkins, 1–10. Maryknoll, NY: Orbis, 1999.

———. Review of *Why, Lord? Suffering and Evil in Black Theology,* by Anthony B. Pinn. *African American Review* 31 (1997) 514–16.

———. *Shoes That Fit Our Feet: Sources for a Constructive Black Theology.* Maryknoll, NY: Orbis, 1993.

Hopkins, Dwight N., and George C. L. Cummings, editors. *Cut Loose Your Stammering Tongue: Black Theology in the Slave Narratives.* 2nd ed. Louisville: Westminster John Knox, 2003.

Hunt, Matthew O., and Larry L. Hunt. "Regional Patterns of African American Church Attendance: Revisiting the Semi-Involuntary Thesis." *Social Forces* 78 (1999) 779–91.

———. "Regional Religions? Extending the 'Semi-Involuntary' Thesis of African-American Religious Participation." *Sociological Forum* 15 (2000) 569–94.

Jacobs, Claude F., and Andrew J. Kaslow. *The Spiritual Churches of New Orleans: Origins, Beliefs, and Rituals of an African-American Religion.* Knoxville: University of Tennessee Press, 1991.

Jacobs, Sylvia M., editor. *Black Americans and the Missionary Movement in Africa.* Contributions in Afro-American and African Studies 66. Westport, CT: Greenwood, 1982.

Jones, William R. *Is God a White Racist? A Preamble to Black Theology.* Boston: Beacon, 1998.

Jordan, Winthrop D. *White over Black: American Attitudes toward the Negro, 1550–1812.* Chapel Hill: University of North Carolina Press, 1968.

Kaufman, Gordon D. *An Essay on Theological Method.* 3rd ed. Reflection and Theory in the Study of Religion 5. Atlanta: Scholars, 1995.

Kelley, Robin D. G. "'Comrades, Praise Gawd for Lenin and Them!': Ideology and Culture among Black Communities in Alabama, 1930–1935." *Science and Society* 52 (1988) 59–82.

Kenyatta, Muhammed Isaiah. "America Was Not Hard to Find." *The Other Side* 93 (1979) 34–42.

Kidwell, Clara Sue, et al. *A Native American Theology.* Maryknoll, NY: Orbis, 2001.

King, Martin Luther, Jr. "The Case against 'Tokenism.'" In *A Testament of Hope: The Essential Writings of Martin Luther King, Jr.,* edited by James Washington, 106–10. New York: HarperCollins, 1986.

———. *Where Do We Go from Here: Chaos or Community?* Boston: Beacon, 1968.

————. *Why We Can't Wait*. In *A Testament of Hope: The Essential Writings of Martin Luther King, Jr.*, edited by James Washington, 518–54. New York: HarperCollins, 1986.

Konieczny, Mary Ellen, and Mark Chaves. "Resources, Race, and Female-Headed Congregations in the United States." *Journal for the Scientific Study of Religion* 39 (2000) 261–71.

Lawrence, Beverly Hall. *Reviving the Spirit: A Generation of African Americans Goes Home to Church*. New York: Grove Press, 1996.

Lee, Jarena. "My All to Preach the Gospel." In *Can I Get a Witness? Prophetic Religious Voices of African American Women, An Anthology*, edited by Marcia Y. Riggs, 6–8. Maryknoll, NY: Orbis, 1997.

Lee, Shayne. *T. D. Jakes: America's New Preacher*. New York: New York University Press, 2005.

Lee, Shayne, and Philip Luke Sinitiere. *Holy Mavericks: Evangelical Innovators and the Spiritual Market Place*. New York: New York University Press, 2009.

Lehman, Edward C., Jr. *Women's Path into Ministry: Six Major Studies*. Pulpit & Pew Research Reports 1. Durham, NC: Duke Divinity School, 2002.

Lincoln, C. Eric, and Lawrence Mamiya. *The Black Church in the African American Experience*. Durham: Duke University Press, 1990.

————. "Daddy Jones and Father Divine: The Cult as Political Religion." *Religion in Life* 49 (1980) 6–23.

Lindbeck, George. *The Nature of Doctrine: Religion and Theology in a Postliberal Age*. Philadelphia: Westminster, 1984.

Long, Charles H. "Interpretations of Black Religion in America." In *Significations: Signs, Symbols, and Images in the Interpretation of Religion*. Minneapolis: Fortress, 1986.

————. "The Oppressive Elements in Religion and the Religions of the Oppressed." In *Significations: Signs, Symbols, and Images in the Interpretation of Religion*. Minneapolis: Fortress, 1986.

Maaga, Mary McCormick. *Hearing the Voices of Jonestown*. Religion and Politics. Syracuse: Syracuse University Press, 1998.

Mamiya, Larry. *River of Struggle, River of Freedom: Trends among Black Churches and Black Pastoral Leadership*. Pulpit & Pew Research Reports. Durham, NC: Duke Divinity School, 2006. Online: http://www.pulpitandpew.duke.edu/DUP&PBlack TrendsWEBfinal!.pdf

Martin, Darnise C. *Beyond Christianity: African Americans in New Thought Church*. Religion, Race, and Ethnicity. New York: New York University Press, 2005.

————. "New Thought." In *Encyclopedia of African American Religious Cultures*, edited by Anthony B. Pinn. Santa Barbara: ABC-CLIO, 2009.

Martin, Joan M. *More Than Chains and Toil: A Christian Work Ethic of Enslaved Women*. Louisville: Westminster John Knox, 2000.

Martin, Waldo, editor. *Brown v. Board of Education: A Brief History with Documents*. The Bedford Series in History and Culture. Boston: Bedford/St. Martin's, 1998.

Matsuoka, Fumitaka. *Out of Silence: Emerging Themes in Asian American Churches*. Cleveland: United Church, 1995.

Mathews, Donald G. "The Southern Rite of Human Sacrifice. Part II: Religion as Punishment." *Journal of Southern Religion* 3 (2000). Online: http://jsr.fsu.edu/mathews2 .htm/.

McElroy, Guy C. "Introduction: Race and Representation." In *Facing History: The Black Image in American Art 1710–1940*, edited by Guy C. McElroy, xi–xxviii. San Francisco: Bedford Arts, 1990.

Michaeli, Ethan. "Another Exodus: The Hebrew Israelites from Chicago to Dimona." In *Black Zion: African American Religious Encounters with Judaism,* edited by Yvonne Chireau and Nathaniel Deutsch, 73–87. Religion in America Series. New York: Oxford University Press, 2000.

Mitchem, Stephanie Y. *Name It and Claim It? Prosperity Preaching in the Black Church.* Cleveland: Pilgrim, 2007.

Moore, Rebecca. *In Defense of Peoples Temple—and Other Essays.* Studies in American Religion 32. Lewiston, NY: Mellen, 1988.

———. *The Jonestown Letters: Correspondence of the Moore Family, 1970–1985.* Studies in American Religion 23. Lewiston, NY: Mellen, 1986.

———. *A Sympathetic History of Jonestown: The Moore Family Involvement in Peoples Temple.* Studies in Religion and Society 14. Lewiston, NY: Mellen, 1985.

Moreno, Paul D. *Black Americans and Organized Labor: A New History.* Baton Rouge: Louisiana State University Press, 2006.

Morris, Aldon, and Dan Clawson. "Lessons of the Civil Rights Movement for Building a Worker Rights Movement." In *Race and Labor: Matters in the New U.S. Economy,* edited by Manning Marable et al, 41–56. Lanham, MD: Rowman & Littlefield, 2006.

Moses, Wilson Jeremiah, editor. *Liberian Dreams: Back-to-Africa Narratives from the 1850s.* University Park: Pennsylvania State University Press, 1998.

Muhammad, Elijah. *The True History of Master Fard Muhammad, Allah (God) in Person.* Compiled and edited by Nasir Makr Hakin Atlanta: MEMPS Publications, 1996.

Murphy, Joseph M. *Working the Spirit: Ceremonies of the African Diaspora.* Boston: Beacon, 1994.

Murray, Pauli. The Pauli Murray Papers. Harvard University, The Schlesinger Library.

———. *Song in a Weary Throat: An American Pilgrimage.* New York: Harper & Row, 1987.

Musick, Marc A. et al. "Race and Formal Volunteering: The Differential Effects of Class and Religion." *Social Forces* 78 (2000) 1539–71.

Official Manual with the Doctrines and Discipline of the Church of God in Christ. Written by the authorization and approval of the General Assembly. Memphis: Church of God in Christ Publishing House, 1973.

Paris, Peter J. *The Social Teaching of the Black Churches.* Philadelphia: Fortress, 1985.

Patterson, James T. *Brown v. Board of Education: A Civil Rights Milestone and Its Troubled Legacy.* Pivotal Moments in American History. New York: Oxford University Press, 2001.

Patterson, Orlando. *Rituals of Blood: Consequences of Slavery in Two American Centuries.* New York: Basic Civitas, 1999.

Patterson, Tiffany Ruby, and Robin D. G. Kelley. "Unfinished Migrations: Reflections on the African Diaspora and the Making of the Modern World." *African Studies Review* 43 (2000) 11–45.

Pearson, Elizabeth Ware, editor. *Letters from Port Royal Written at the Time of the Civil War.* Boston: Clarke, 1906.

Pinn, Anthony B. *African American Humanist Principles: Living and Thinking Like the Children of Nimrod.* Black Religion, Womanist Thought, Social Justice. New York: Palgrave Macmillan, 2004.

———. "A Beautiful *Be-ing*: Religious Humanism and the Aesthetics of a New Salvation." In *Black Religion and Aesthetics: Religious Thought and Life in Africa and the African Diaspora,* edited by Anthony B. Pinn, 19–36. New York: Palgrave Macmillan, 2009.

————. *Becoming "America's Problem Child": An Outline of Pauli Murray's Religious Life and Theology*. Eugene, OR: Pickwick Publications, 2007.

————. *The Black Church in the Post–Civil Rights Era*. Maryknoll, NY: Orbis, 2002.

————, editor. *By These Hands: A Documentary History of African American Humanism*. New York: New York University Press, 2001.

————. *Embodiment and the New Shape of Black Theological Thought*. New York: New York University Press, forthcoming.

————. "Embracing Nimrod's Legacy: The Irreverence of Fantasy and the Redemption of Black Theology." In *Loving the Body: Black Religious Studies and the Erotic*, edited by Anthony B. Pinn and Dwight N. Hopkins, 157–78. Black Religion, Womanist Thought, Social Justice. New York: Palgrave Macmillan, 2004.

————. "Facing Competing Claims: Thoughts on a Theory of Theological Discourse." *Theological Education* 38 (2002) 87–95.

————. "Getting Wright Wrong: Preaching Is Not Policy." *Religion Dispatches*, April 3, 2008. Online: http://www.religiondispatches.org/archive/election08/163/getting_wright_wrong%3A_preaching_is_not_policy/.

————. "Inauguration Day: Re-imagining Ourselves." *Religion Dispatches*, January 2009. Online: http://www.religiondispatches.org/archive/election08/929/inauguration _day%3A_re-imagining_ourselves/.

————. "Introduction: The Black Labyrinth, Aesthetics, and Black Religion." In *Black Religion and Aesthetics: Religious Thought and Life in Africa and the African Diaspora*, edited by Anthony B. Pinn, 1–18. New York: Palgrave Macmillan, 2009.

————. "Keep on Keepin' On: Reflections on 'Get On the Bus' and the Language of Movement." In *Black Religion after the Million-Man March: Voices on the Future*, edited by Garth Kasimu Baker-Fletcher, 58–67. Maryknoll, NY: Orbis, 1998.

————. "King and the Civil Rights Movement: Thoughts on the Aesthetics of Social Transformation." In *Companion to Martin Luther King, Jr.*, edited by Robert Franklin and Timothy Jackson. Cambridge University Press, forthcoming.

————. "Like Prophets and Disciples: Is There a Gap between the Academy and the Church?" *The AME Church Review* 119 (2003) 79–82.

————. "Making a World with a Beat: Musical Expression's Relationship to Religious Identity and Experience." In *Noise and Spirit : The Religious and Spiritual Sensibilities of Rap Music*, edited by Anthony B. Pinn, 1–26. New York: New York University Press, 2003.

————. "New Religious Movements in Global Perspective: Views from the Mainstream." *Reviews in Religion and Theology* 7 (2000) 145–50.

————. "On a Mission from God: African American Music and the Nature/Meaning of Conversion and Religious Life." In *Between Sacred and Profane: Researching Religion and Popular Culture*, edited by Gordon Lynch, 143–57. London: Tauris, 2007.

————. "O(Pinn)ion: Reevaluating a Faith-Based Nation." *Religion Dispatches*, February 13, 2009. Online: http://www.religiondispatches.org/archive/politics/1079/o(pinn)ion%3A_reevaluating_a_faith-based_nation_/.

————, editor. *Pauli Murray: Selected Sermons and Writings*. Maryknoll, NY: Orbis, 2006.

————. "Peoples Temple as Black Religion: Re-Imagining the Contours of Black Religious Studies." In *Peoples Temple and Black Religion in America*, edited by Rebecca Moore et al., 1–27. Bloomington: Indiana University Press, 2004.

————. Review of *How Race Is Made*, by Mark Smith; *Being Human*, by Dwight Hopkins; *What's Faith Got to Do With It?* by Kelly Brown Douglas; and *Colored Pictures*, by Michael Harris. *Religious Studies Review* 33 (2007) 1–8.

———. "Sweaty Bodies in a Circle: Thoughts on the Subtle Dimensions of Black Religion as Protest." *Black Theology* 4 (2006) 11–26.

———. *Terror and Triumph: The Nature of Black Religion*. Minneapolis: Fortress, 2003.

———. *Varieties of African American Religious Experience*. Minneapolis: Fortress, 1998.

———. *Why, Lord? Suffering and Evil in Black Theology*. New York: Continuum, 1995.

———. "William R. Jones and Religiously Justified Conduct: Personal Reflections." *Religious Humanism*, forthcoming.

Pitts, Walter F. *Old Ship of Zion: The Afro-Baptist Ritual in the African Diaspora*. Religion in America Series. New York: Oxford University Press, 1996.

Portmann, John. *In Defense of Sin*. New York: Palgrave for St. Martin's, 2001.

Raboteau, Albert. *Slave Religion: The "Invisible Institution" in the Antebellum South*. Updated ed. New York: Oxford University Press, 2004.

Randolph, Florence Spearing. "Antipathy to Women Preachers." In *Daughters of Thunder: Black Women Preachers and Their Sermons, 1850–1979*, edited by Bettye Collier-Thomas. San Francisco: Jossey-Bass, 1998.

Rasor, Stephen C., and Christine D. Chapman. *Black Power from the Pew: Laity Connecting Congregations and Communities*. Cleveland: Pilgrim, 2007.

Rauschenbuch, Walter. *Christianity and the Social Crisis*. New York: Macmillan, 1907.

———. *A Theology for the Social Gospel*. New York: Macmillan, 1917.

Redkey, Edwin S. *Black Exodus: Black Nationalist and Back-to-Africa Movements, 1890–1910*. Yale Publications in American Studies 17. New Haven: Yale University Press, 1969.

———, editor and compiler. *Respect Black: The Writings and Speeches of Henry McNeal Turner*. The American Negro, His History and Literature. New York: Arno, 1971.

Reese, Laura A., and Ronald E. Brown. "The Effects of Religious Messages on Racial Identity and System Blame among African Americans." *The Journal of Politics* 57 (1995) 24–43.

Riggs, Marcia Y., editor. *Can I Get a Witness? Prophetic Religious Voices of African American Women: An Anthology*. Maryknoll, NY: Orbis, 1997.

Ruether, Rosemary Radford. *Sexism and God-Talk: Toward a Feminist Theology*. Boston: Beacon, 1993.

Sahgal, Neha, and Greg Smith. "A Religious Portrait of African Americans." *Pew Research Center's Forum on Religion & Public Life*. January 30, 2009. Online: http://pewforum.org/docs/?DocID=389/.

Saliba, John A. *Christian Responses to the New Age Movement: A Critical Assessment*. London: Chapman, 1999.

Sawyer, Mary R. "'My Lord, What a Mourning:' Twenty Years Since Jonestown." Online: http://jonestown.sdsu.edu/AboutJonestown/Articles/sawyer.htm/.

Sernett, Milton C. *Bound for the Promised Land: Black Religion and the Great Migration*. C. Eric Lincoln Series on the Black Experience. Durham: Duke University Press, 2000.

Smith, Archie, Jr. "An Interpretation of the Peoples Temple and Jonestown: Implications for the Black Church." PSR Bulletin Occasional Paper 58 (1980) no. 2. Reprinted in *People's Temple and Black Religion in America*, edited by Rebecca Moore, et al., 47–56. Bloomington: Indiana University Press, 2004.

———. "We Need to Press Forward: Black Religion and Jonestown, Twenty Years Later." Online: http://jonestown.sdsu.edu/AboutJonestown/Articles/smith.htm/.

Smith, J. Alfred, Sr. "Black Theology and the Parish Ministry." In *Black Faith and Public Talk: Critical Essays on James H. Cone's "Black Theology and Black Power,"* edited by Dwight Hopkins, 89–95. Maryknoll, NY: Orbis, 1999.

Smith, Mark M. *How Race Is Made: Slavery, Segregation, and the Senses.* Chapel Hill: University of North Carolina Press, 2006.

Smith, Jonathan Z. *Map Is Not Territory: Studies in the History of Religions.* 1978. Reprinted, Chicago: University of Chicago Press, 1993.

Smith, Theophus H. *Conjuring Culture: Biblical Formations of Black America.* Religion in America Series. New York: Oxford University Press, 1994.

Spiritual Workshop. "Didn't My Lord Deliver Daniel." Online: http://www.negrospirituals .com/news-song/didn_t_my_lord_delier_daniel.htm.

Stewart, Maria W. *Maria W. Stewart, America's First Black Woman Political Writer: Essays and Speeches,* edited and introduced by Marilyn Richardson. Blacks in the Diaspora. Bloomington: Indiana University Press, 1987.

Stuckey, Sterling. *Slave Culture: Nationalist Theory and the Foundations of Black America.* New York: Oxford University Press, 1987.

Taylor, Cynthia. *A. Philip Randolph: The Religious Journey of an African American Labor Leader.* New York: New York University Press, 2006.

Terrell, Joanne Marie. *Power in the Blood? The Cross in the African American Experience.* The Bishop Henry McNeal Turner/Sojourner Truth Series in Black Religion 15. Maryknoll, NY: Orbis, 1998.

Thurman, Howard. *Deep Is the Hunger: Meditations for Apostles of Sensitiveness.* Richmond, IN: Friends United Press, 1978.

———. *The Inward Journey.* Richmond, IN: Friends United Press, 1996.

———. *Jesus and the Disinherited.* Boston: Beacon, 1996.

———. *The Luminous Darkness: A Personal Interpretation of the Anatomy of Segregation and the Ground of Hope.* New York: Harper & Row, 1965.

———. *With Head and Heart: The Autobiography of Howard Thurman.* New York: Harcourt Brace Jovanovich, 1979.

Walton, Jonathan L. *Watch This! The Ethics and Aesthetics of Black Televangelism.* Religion, Race, and Ethnicity. New York: New York University Press, 2009.

Washington, James M., editor. *A Testament of Hope: The Essential Writings of Martin Luther King, Jr.* New York: Harper & Row, 1986.

Washington, Joseph. "How Black is Black Religion?" In *Quest for a Black Theology*, edited by James J. Gardiner and J. Deotis Roberts, 22ff. Philadelphia: Pilgrim 1971.

Weightman, Judith Mary. *Making Sense of the Jonestown Suicides: A Sociological History of Peoples Temple.* Studies in Reilgion and Society 7. New York: Mellen, 1983.

Welch, Sharon D. *A Feminist Ethic of Risk.* Minneapolis: Fortress, 2000.

———. "Frustration and Righteous Anger Do Not a Politics Make." In *Sweet Dreams in America: Making Ethics and Spirituality Work,* 27–52. New York: Routledge, 1999.

Wessinger, Catherine. *How the Millennium Comes Violently: From Jonestown to Heaven's Gate.* New York: Seven Bridges, 2000.

West, Cornel. *Prophesy Deliverance! An Afro-American Revolutionary Christianity.* 20th anniversary ed., with a new preface by the author. Louisville: Westminster John Knox, 2002.

———. "Prophetic Christian as Organic Intellectual: Martin Luther King, Jr." In *The Cornel West Reader,* edited by Cornel West, 425–34. New York: Basic Civitas, 1999.

———. *Race Matters.* New York: Vintage, 1994.

―――. "Subversive Joy and Revolutionary Patience in Black Christianity." In *The Cornel West Reader*, edited by Cornel West, 435–40. New York: Basic Civitas, 1999.

White, Shane, and Graham White. *Stylin': African American Expressive Culture from Its Beginnings to the Zoot Suit*. Ithaca: Cornell University Press, 1998.

Wiggins, Daphne C. *Righteous Content: Black Women's Perspectives of Church and Faith*. Religion, Race, and Ethnicity. New York: New York University Press, 2005.

Williams, Delores S. *Sisters in the Wilderness: The Challenge of Womanist God-Talk*. Maryknoll, NY: Orbis, 1993.

Williams, Melvin D. *Community in a Black Pentecostal Church: An Anthropological Study*. Pittsburgh: University of Pittsburgh Press, 1974.

Wilmore, Gayraud S., editor. *African American Religious Studies: An Interdisciplinary Anthology*. Durham: Duke University Press, 1989.

―――. *Black Religion and Black Radicalism: An Interpretation of the Religious History of Afro-American People*. Maryknoll, NY: Orbis, 1983.

Wilson, Bryan, and Jamie Cresswell. *New Religious Movements: Challenge and Response*. London: Routledge, in association with the Institute of Oriental Philosophy European Centre, 1999.

Wright, Richard. *Black Boy (American Hunger): A Record of Childhood and Youth*. New York: Harper Perennial Modern Classics, 2008.

Zepp, Ira G., Jr. *The New Religious Image of Urban America: The Shopping Mall as Ceremonial Center*. Niwot, CO: University Press of Colorado, 1997.

Index of Names